The Age of a Spider Monkey

And Other Revelations from the Back of a Zoo

The Age of a
Spider Monkey

And Other Revelations from
the Back of a Zoo

Jeanie K. Bailey

The Age of a Spider Monkey
And Other Revelations from the Back of a Zoo

First Printing, June 2022

Printed in the United States of America

Dedication

To Monkers, an affectionate spider monkey with a penchant for belly rubs. He spent his life in captivity, never experiencing the freedom of choosing his companions, the foods he'd like to eat, or his living environment. All of those things were chosen for him by the human system that owned him. May we do better.

Author's Note

This is my story, and I do not intend for my words to speak for others. For that reason, I have changed the names of the people, the zoo, and most of the animals. I have created composite conversations and situations in order to protect the privacy of those who share my story with me. The incidents involving animals and the behind-the-scenes activities at the zoo are true to the best of my knowledge and memory.

Table of Contents

Preface

Animals are such agreeable friends–they ask no
questions, they pass no criticisms.
– George Eliot

I was born in the 1960s, the youngest of seven
children, at a time when families with lots of
kids were not uncommon, though usually because
they were Catholic. That wasn't the case for us.
According to my mom, she and my father were just
really bad at birth control. Unlike her two sisters,
her family struggled financially — no doubt because
of its large size. We did not have much money, but
we had lots of love and a great support system.

Like most families back then, we had a dog who
spent all of his time outside. King was adored by
all of us, yet not treated to the evolved standards of
today. Since I was the "animal lover" of the family,
my mom also allowed me to acquire any pet that
I wanted. Over the years, I had cats, mice, turtles,
birds, rabbits, gerbils, and guinea pigs. I considered
my animals to be family and often felt more
comfortable and connected to them than to humans.
My family also frequented the local zoo.

At the age of twenty-two, I started volunteering
at the same zoo that I had visited for all those years
of my childhood, and I continued to volunteer off-
and-on for the next nine years.

Though it has been more than twenty years since I
last mucked a stall in a barn or scratched the belly of

a spider monkey, the things I learned about animals and about what happens behind the scenes at zoos have stayed with me and helped inform my view of how all animals should be treated. For that, I will always be grateful.

– Jeanie K. Bailey

Part One: The Beginning

Until one has loved an animal, a part of
one's soul remains unawakened.
— Anatole France

Orientation

Do not wait until the conditions are
perfect to begin. Beginning makes the
conditions perfect.
— Alan Cohen

It was still chilly in early spring. I was nervously driving my car to the downtown area of a neighboring city. I knew my way around the zoo, but getting there was another matter. I hadn't done a lot of driving in traffic as I'd spent my teen years out in the country and had learned to drive on winding ditch-lined roads without a lot of other cars around. I could fly around a country curve but put me on the interstate and my palms would start to sweat.

I was both relieved and excited when I arrived at the building designated for the zoo's volunteer orientation. I could hardly believe it was happening. I felt as though I'd grown up here, interacting with all of the animals at the zoo and dreaming of one day becoming a zookeeper . . . or perhaps a veterinarian ... I couldn't decide. I just knew that I wanted to help animals. Arriving in the parking lot of that huge building—the one marked "Zoo Administration" and designated for "Staff Only"—was as close to that dream as I had ever been.

As I walked up to the building, I was still marveling that I was going to be allowed inside. This place had been a mystery to me all my life. I'd seen it many times on my visits to the zoo but had never understood its purpose. What did they do in there?

A woman at the front desk directed me to a room on the second floor. Once I made my way up the stairs and down a corridor that reminded me of high school, I was greeted by a blonde woman dressed in the brown khaki uniform of a zookeeper. She asked, "Are you here for the orientation?"

I smiled and wondered if she could see my lips quivering with nervousness, "Yes."

"Great, I'm Monica. I hope you remembered to bring your $20.00 registration fee?" She raised her eyebrows in question, and I got the feeling the registration fee was an issue with some volunteers.

"I have it," I said.

"I need you to fill out these forms," she said as she matter-of-factly handed me a clipboard and a pen. "You can have a seat anywhere you like," she waved me into a classroom while she remained at the door to greet other arrivals.

I chose a desk in the front. I was all-in and didn't want to miss one second of orientation.

As I gazed down at the forms, I learned there were multiple ways you could volunteer. I hoped I'd be able to choose a position that interacted with animals.

The first form asked me for my areas of interest: Docents, Horticulture, or Zookeeper Assistant. Well, that turned out to be a no-brainer for me. First, I didn't know what a "Docent" was (I would learn about that later)—what I did know was that I wanted to work with animals and with zookeepers, so assisting them would be perfect. "Zookeeper Assistant, check," I whispered to myself as I marked my choice, not yet knowing what a profound education awaited me.

Monkey Business

We read our children stories starring
elephants and monkeys and bears to teach
them about nobility, curiosity and courage . . .
— Lydia Millet

It was an early Saturday morning, and the weather was brisk and sunny. I had butterflies in my stomach. Like a child on Christmas Eve, I had a hard time sleeping the night before. I was about to start my first day as a volunteer Zookeeper Assistant, and I couldn't stop myself from smiling. I had dressed in the red polo shirt they gave me at the end of orientation. Presumably the reason for the $20 registration fee. It read, "VOLUNTEER" in all caps and had the zoo logo on it. It made me feel very official. I had pulled on a pair of jeans and tennis shoes and applied makeup as well. I wanted to look my best and had not yet discovered what a dirty job I had ahead of me. I was full of excitement and nervousness as I puffed on a cigarette and drove with the sunrise at my back.

I had left my sleeping boyfriend Brad's apartment way too early, I knew. He lived in the same city as the zoo, and he and I had already practiced the drive. It should only take me ten minutes, but I wasn't taking any chances and had left at 6:30 that morning for a 7 a.m. arrival time. As I pulled into the parking lot, I drove past the section designated for the public. I'm not the "public" anymore, I thought, as I kept driving toward the back gate. I could see from my car that the gate had a big padlock on it. I parked and waited, and waited some more.

Just as I was wondering if I should get out of my car and stand at the gate, I saw a zookeeper approaching the fence. At least, I assumed he was a zookeeper. I hadn't officially met anyone besides Monica, but this guy had on the uniform and was unlocking the padlock. I jumped out of my car and rushed over to him. He was tall and handsome with shoulder-length dirty-blond hair and a set of multiple keys in his hand. I estimated he was in his late twenties or early thirties. He glanced over and gave me a nod as he pulled the vehicle-sized gate open just wide enough to fit us humans.

"First day?" He asked.

I nodded.

"You'll want to head over to the kitchen," he said, pointing to the red wooden building with a screened back porch and a door marked, simply, "Kitchen."

"Thanks," I smiled back. He didn't introduce himself, but I'd find out later that he was Matt, and he worked with the elephants.

I walked through the screened-in porch area that held a shelf full of walkie-talkies; zookeeper jackets hung on hooks below them and boots were tucked under a long wooden bench. I stepped hesitantly into the kitchen, unsure where I was supposed to go. It was already bustling with activity — a swarm of keepers in khaki uniforms and volunteers in red polos. I saw a familiar face across the large kitchen island and headed her way.

"Hi, Monica," I said when I reached her.

Monica's face held a look of annoyance as she stuck her pen in her mouth and flipped the page on her clipboard. "What was your name again?" she muttered between occupied teeth.

"Jeanie," I said, "Jeanie Bailey."

"Oh right . . ." she found me on her list and popped the pen out of her mouth to mark the page. "Okay . . . Jeanie, you're with Lisa today. Lisa's with the monkeys. Do you know where that is?" I nodded. "Good, head on over there, and she'll put you to work."

I started to go out the way I had come, but she directed me to the front, a shortcut that would put me in a direct line for a building dubbed monkey house.

I had to walk through the barnyard area and past the cafe. It was a peaceful walk. I had never before seen the zoo empty of visitors and that calm atmosphere in the early morning hours would become my favorite time of day. There was no one around to drown out the sounds of bleating sheep and goats and the haunting call of what I knew to be a gibbon. The barnyard animals approached the fence as I walked past them, probably hoping for a kibble handout. There was a feeder attached to the fencepost; visitors could insert quarters and receive bits of feed to offer to the animals. As a visitor in the past, I used to feed them all the time. All I could offer at the moment was a pat on the head.

As I got past the barnyard, the bison yard came into my sight on the right. Five huge majestic animals were grazing in a field covered with fog that made it look like they were walking on clouds.

Again I heard the exotic whooping sound of the gibbon. If I didn't already have my eye on the building, those calls would alert me that I'm getting close. The monkey yards were fenced in around a central building that housed their indoor enclosures. The whole site had a larger fence surrounding it to keep zoo-goers from having direct contact with the animals. If they stuck their fingers into the outer fence, there would still be a good two feet between their knuckles and the monkeys' inner fence. As I approached, I could see that the outer gate was wide open. I took that as an invitation and stepped inside as I called, "Hello? Lisa?"

Lisa was a short-haired brunette woman of small stature with a ready smile and a firm handshake. At five feet eight inches tall, I towered over her. She greeted me heartedly as I told her my name, and she seemed genuinely grateful for my presence.

"I'm so happy to have a volunteer!" she said. "And I'm not just saying that; I can't do my job without your help. How often can you come?"

She was so friendly and enthusiastic, I couldn't help but return her smile as I assured her, "I'm hoping to come every Saturday."

"Perfect," she said. "Whatever time you can give is appreciated. I had a regular volunteer, but she moved out of state recently. Navy wife," she said by way of explanation.

We lived in a transient area that was home to large military bases. Families were often coming and going and the term "Navy wife" was common.

"Okay, let's get you started. Do you want to meet some monkeys?" she asked with a sheepish grin. I nodded and followed as she quickly moved into the secured back area.

We passed by indoor housing that was divided into three sections. Each unit had food dishes and water bottles, ropes for swinging and hanging on, and platforms for lying down. At the moment, there were no monkeys to be seen.

Lisa gestured for me to continue following her, "Come outside, and I'll introduce you," she said as we kept walking and stepped through to the outer section surrounding the monkey yard.

"This here is Monkers," she said, referring to the largest spider monkey who had rushed over to greet her, pressing his little belly up against the fence. Lisa cooed at him while she scratched his belly, "Who's my little Monk-Monk?" She obviously had a soft spot for this handsome fella.

"Monkers is about twenty-two years old," she said, glancing over at me to see my reaction.

"Wait, twenty-two? He's my age!" I told her.

I couldn't wrap my brain around the fact that this little monkey had probably been living in a zoo as long as I had been living, period. I didn't know if he had been born here or captured in the wild, which had only just dawned on me with the simple knowledge of his age. I wasn't sure which was worse, having freedom and losing it, or never having discovered it at all.

"Has he always been at this zoo?" I asked timidly as I wasn't sure how open she would be to answering my questions, or how open I would be to hearing her answers.

"I'm not sure..." she hesitated, "but he's the oldest spider monkey I've ever met. I've only been here a few years though," she said with an afterthought. "You want to scratch him?"

"Yes, absolutely," I replied as I reached out and began rubbing his soft belly fur. He loved the attention, and as he pressed himself up against the fence he made soft grunting noises. Lisa said she thought he was "taken" with me. I hoped so. I was certainly taken with him.

I met all of the other spider monkeys, but it was hard to keep track of their names. I told myself that I'd remember better over time, and I did. The one that stood out from the rest, besides old Monkers, was Rosie. She was pregnant.

"So they let them have babies here?" I asked.

"We don't prevent pregnancies," she said. "Babies are great for bringing crowds to the zoo," she added for explanation. "We'll even put animals together to encourage them to mate. Sometimes it doesn't work out. Mating isn't always a sure thing, or if it happens, the mothers aren't always able to raise their young. Animals born in captivity may not know what to do for their young, because they were never taught. The mom might not feed her baby, or the dad might attack their young. In Rosie's case, Monkers is the father, and he's done well with his offspring in the past. The other male monkey, Reggie, is not yet old enough to challenge Monkers. That may happen someday though, and we don't know what kind of father he'll be."

"What happens if it doesn't work out?" I asked. "I mean for the babies and their parents?"

"We'll separate the young and raise them ourselves. Usually one of the keepers will help by taking them home for nightly feedings. Then we either reintroduce them when they're older or sell them to another zoo," she explained.

I hadn't ever thought of that—zoos selling animals to other zoos. It seemed a lot of what I was learning had never occurred to me before.

"Have you seen the gibbons?" she asked.

"Only on visits to the zoo; I mean, not as a volunteer," I explained.

She directed me to the other side of the building where two gibbons were swinging from branches scattered around an outdoor enclosure. The female, Sasha, was a beautiful golden color; and the male, Rufus, was black. "I know we call this monkey house, but gibbons are apes, not monkeys," Lisa informed me, and I could tell she enjoyed educating her volunteers.

"Oh, I didn't realize that… what's the difference?" I asked.

"The biggest difference that you can easily see is that monkeys have long tails, and apes don't," she explained. "Did you ever notice this little guy is missing part of his arm?" she asked, pointing to Rufus.

"Yes, I did. I always wondered what happened to him. Was he born that way?" I asked.

"Oh no, it happened at another zoo. See those doors that lead inside?" she pointed to the rectangular entrance to the indoor enclosure, and I nodded. "They close like a guillotine," she karate chopped her right hand into her left palm, and I flinched. "At the other zoo, there was a malfunction, and a door like that one slammed down on his arm as he was going through it. Chopped the bottom half of his arm right off," she stated it in such a matter-of-fact way, I could tell some of the horror of what had happened had faded for her. Perhaps from telling the story so often.

"That's just terrible," I stammered.

"I know, but he doesn't seem to have a problem getting around now," she said apologetically. We both turned to watch Rufus swinging around the yard, going from hand to foot and back again.

"That can't happen here; we have sensors to

prevent it—you know how elevator doors won't close on you? It's like that," she added.

Well, that's a relief, I thought.

"Okay, we need to get started, we're really behind now. Come inside, and I'll show you how to clean. You can do spider monkeys while I take care of gibbons," she directed me to the interior.

As Lisa instructed me on my tasks—emptying their bowls of old monkey biscuits, changing out their water, sweeping then scrubbing the floor with a push broom and a bleach mixture—I took it all in, anxious to get started. As soon as I began my work, she left me on my own.

Lisa explained that the routine I was going through is performed every morning at 7 a.m., every single day of the week. I was surprised at how dirty the place could get in just twenty-four hours. I wondered how she accomplished all of the work on weekdays when fewer volunteers were available and planned to ask her later.

I had finished the first pen and went to empty the monkey bowl in the second enclosure, but stopped cold. Sitting pretty as you please on top of a pile of monkey biscuits, with long twitchy antennae, was the largest cockroach I had ever seen. I jumped back. I didn't know bugs of this size existed in our area! It was two or three inches of terror, and I was not a fan. For a few minutes, I stood outside the enclosure wondering what the heck I was going to do. I had a serious cockroach phobia that I was only now beginning to fully discover. I didn't want to ask Lisa for help so soon—this was my first assignment. I wanted her to trust me to get the work done. I would have to deal with it myself. Crap.

I tried to walk past the bowl to get inside and

clean. I'm just going to ignore it, I thought. But in reality, I couldn't make it past the doorway. Trapped in a cage, even a large one, with a giant cockroach? No, thank you. I was too freaked out.

Then I remembered the hose. The "firehose," as Lisa called it, looks just like it sounds. It's huge, and it packs a powerful punch of water. I was supposed to be using it to rinse after scrubbing, but this little problem was costing me time. I turned behind me to the spool of hose hanging on the wall and unwound it. Aiming for the food container, I turned the valve just as Lisa had shown me, and a blast of water sent old monkey biscuits and one giant cockroach skyrocketing across the room. I had to balance myself to keep from falling backward. I used the stream of water to force the biscuits and the bug to the edge of the enclosure and down into a ditch bordering the cement floor that eventually led to a big drainage hole at the end.

Lisa must have heard the water as she came hurrying back into the room.

"Are you done already?" she asked with a strained look on her face that said I certainly shouldn't be. It was far too early for me to be using the hose.

"No," I replied sheepishly, embarrassed to relay what happened. "There was a giant cockroach on the monkey biscuits and . . . "

She interrupted me with laughter and patted me on the arm, "Oh, that! Happens all the time, and I do the same thing! Hit 'em with the hose, good thinking!" She winked at me. "Are you good to go now?" she asked. I nodded and she made a quick exit to continue her work on the other side of monkey house.

And that was the first of countless times that I

would use a firehose to deal with a cockroach.

* * *

Once we had cleaned monkey house, we rushed over to the kitchen to prepare meals. The monkeys were to receive a specific amount of fruits and greens along with their monkey chow biscuits. Lisa took me through the kitchen, exiting the screened porch to the back. This was the same back area I had come through after entering the gate that morning. We turned right toward a walk-in refrigerator. It was huge, and it housed everything from meats and birdseed to fruits and vegetables. I helped to gather the items from Lisa's list and carried them back to the kitchen island — a large square that took up most of the room and allowed for multiple people to prep food at the same time.

Lisa handed me a sharp knife and a metal glove. "You have to wear this. Insurance," she said simply, as if that one word explained everything.

I stared at the mesh glove as if it were a foreign object; for me, it was. Then she added, "It will keep you from cutting yourself."

While she went back to the walk-in to measure out the monkey chow, I chopped the fruit with my right hand while my left was protected by the glove. Pretty ingenious, I thought. Would be nice to have one at home. I was surprised by how quickly I took to the task. From that day forward, food prep became one of my favorite duties at the zoo — second only to interacting with the animals.

Across the island was an older volunteer — I thought she might be in her late thirties or early forties. She had long, brown hair and a face clear of makeup. She wore a Pittsburgh Steelers jacket over her red polo so I assumed she was from Pennsylvania, which was pretty common in our area. I had seen her piling food into a cart when we exited the walk-in.

"Hi, I'm Jeanie," I introduced myself.

"I'm Jan, nice to meet you," she replied.

"Have you been here long?" I asked.

"Going on five years," she said proudly.

Five years seemed like both an eternity and an inspiration. "Who are you prepping food for?" I gestured to the pile in front of her.

"The elephants. And boy do they eat a lot!" she laughed. "We're also putting a dozen bales of hay on the truck. And they told me today that I could help wash them, I've never done that before," she confided, and I could tell she was excited about it.

"How do you wash an elephant?" I couldn't help but laugh too.

"Like a car!" She exclaimed. "When they kneel on the floor, they're about the same size and shape as a Volkswagen bug. I've watched them do it, but they've never allowed a volunteer to help before. I guess I'll be the first," she said proudly.

"Well congratulations, that sounds exciting," I told her. I was thinking about my first car, which was a VW bug. Maybe if I'm here long enough, I thought, I'll get to wash elephants too.

Jan finished her food prep before I did; there wasn't a lot of chopping to do for elephants, just counting and sorting. As she made her exit, Lisa returned. We took our measured amounts of food to a golf cart-style vehicle where she had been busy loading the back with other items. Once we returned to monkey house, I distributed half the goodies to their bowls, saving the other half for their outdoor yard where Lisa planned to hide it for them. She said it would give the monkeys something to do and help to stimulate their minds and prevent boredom. She called it "enrichment." In their wild habitat in South America, spider monkeys rarely leave the trees. When gathering their food, they hang from their tails, which are sometimes longer than their bodies. They hold onto tree limbs and swing around grabbing at food with their hands. Lisa wanted to provide them with as much natural movement as possible, sticking the food in places that they could only swing on their tails to reach.

Once the food was placed indoors, the guillotine doors were opened, and the monkeys came rushing in. It was obvious that they knew it was time to eat. We counted every monkey before re-closing the doors. I couldn't help but cringe thinking about what had happened to the male gibbon's arm.

I wanted to hang out with the spider monkeys a little longer. I was fascinated by the way they peeled and ate their fruit, and Monkers had let me scratch his belly again. But we had more work to do and proceeded to the outdoor enclosures.

Lisa handed me a rake and started placing the food around their yard as I began my task of cleaning. It was fairly easy work in the cool spring weather, raking monkey poop and discarded fruit peels while chatting with her.

"How do you handle all of this work when you don't have a volunteer?" I asked her.

"I share the work with another keeper, or everything will just run late. I usually have at least one volunteer on the weekends, and during the week the zoo is slower and the crowds aren't here as early so there's not as much of a rush to get the work done," she explained.

We talked more about animals and life in general, and the more we talked, the more I liked her. She was strong and independent and obviously cared about animals. I asked about how she came to be at the zoo.

"I moved from South Carolina for this job. I majored in biology and worked at a state park, but what I really wanted to do was work with animals," she said. "It doesn't pay well . . ." she continued. "But it's worth it."

The Raptors Have to Eat

A free bird leaps
on the back of the wind
and floats downstream
till the current ends
and dips his wing
in the orange sun rays
and dares to claim the sky.
— Maya Angelou, *Caged Bird*

While we were talking, Lisa filled me in on the other animals on our "string."

"Each keeper is responsible for their string," she explained. "String 5 is my string, and it includes the monkeys, the sea lion, the raptors, the duck pond, and the docent animals. When you work with me, you'll work in all of those areas," she said.

"What is a raptor?" I asked.

"A raptor is a bird of prey—that means they eat prey animals. We have barn owls, golden eagles, and a falcon. They're over on the other side of the pond," she pointed.

"Oh right, I know where they are, I just didn't know they were called raptors," I replied. That was a section of the zoo that I didn't visit too often. I liked the mammals and spent a lot of time with the monkeys and elephants. The birds of prey were right next to the sea lion, though, so I saw them on the way there on occasion. They weren't very active and didn't stimulate my interest at the time.

I thought it was odd that the zoo seemed to base its animal care "strings" by location rather than by the type of animal. I would have thought there would be keepers with specialties, so I asked Lisa what kind of schooling you needed to be a keeper.

"The job requirement says 'high school diploma,'" she used her hands to make air quotes and could see by my expression how much that surprised me. "I don't know if you realize it, but we actually work for the city. We're glorified janitors."

"But didn't you say you have a Bachelor's in biology, and you moved here for this job?" I asked.

"Yes, and yes. I moved for the job, not the pay!" she laughed.

We drove our cart past the pond and up to the row of raptor enclosures. They looked like giant bird cages.

We approached the first one, housing two golden eagles, and Lisa turned back toward the cart. It never occurred to me before, but as I looked up at the birds roosting at the top of the cage, I realized the cage roof prevented them from seeing the sky. No wonder they weren't very active. No sky to ponder, no room to spread your wings—an animal that is meant to soar can do nothing more than hop from limb to limb. I shook the disturbing thought from my mind and focused on the task at hand.

"Do you want me to grab the seed?" I asked, referring to one of the buckets she had put into our cart.

She gave a soft laugh, "No honey, these are birds of prey. They don't eat seeds."

"Oh, right. Well . . . what are you feeding them?" I asked, almost afraid of the answer.

"Usually we feed them rodents. Rodents, pigeons,

rabbits, and chicken parts… sometimes baby chicks," she looked at me waiting for a reaction.

I had never thought about it before.

"Where do you get their food?" I asked slowly because the words didn't want to come out of my mouth.

"We buy some of it, and . . . we raise some of it," she said slowly and softly. "The mice and rats are in the back of the exhibit building, the guinea pigs and rabbits are in hutches outside the exhibit building, and the chicks are hatched in the barnyard," she answered.

The exhibit building, which the zookeepers call the EB for short, held small animals, reptiles, and nocturnal animals. Because of the nocturnal animals, half of the building was kept in the dark. The back area was the area behind the public displays accessible only to employees and volunteers. I didn't realize there was an outdoor area behind the exhibit building, also not in the public eye.

"We bonk them behind the building then bring them over here freshly dead," she continued.

I gulped. "Uh . . . what does bonk mean?" I really didn't want to know, and it felt like a dark cloud had settled over us.

"It's how we kill them," she said quietly. "There are two ways. We have a drowning trap, you probably walked right by it when you entered the kitchen. It's a metal bucket with a cage inside. You put the animal in the cage, fill the bucket up with water, then put the cage in the bucket. . ." she was watching me carefully. "It's been suggested that we not use that anymore," she paused. "So. . . now we put them in a plastic bag, and then swing it and slam it on a hard surface. That's called bonking, and it's the least cruel method. They die instantly," she stopped talking for a minute. "At least that's the idea ... drowning takes ... time," she looked away before turning back to the cart.

I stood there for a few moments in shock. So many thoughts were running through my mind, and some of them conflicted with each other. How could they do that? I wondered. But they were zookeepers, didn't they love animals? Of course they did, but ... I could never do that... does that mean I could never be a zookeeper? What was I thinking? They had to feed the raptors, right? The raptors have to eat. . . Wait, oh my God, what do they feed all of the other carnivores? And the snakes? And... oh my God. I didn't want to know. I felt a little sick, but Lisa had moved on, and I needed to join her.

"It's better than feeding the animals to them alive, you know? Bonking?" she said quietly, then abruptly turned away again. I got the impression I was making her feel guilty. Maybe my innocence was reminding her of a way of thinking that she had lost.

She pulled something that looked like a welder's mask out from under the golf-cart seat and held it for me to see. She laughed at my look of confusion and instantly the tension broke.

"These birds are no joke. I have to protect myself," she winked and pulled the mask over her head. Now I could see it wasn't a welder's mask after all but a sturdy leather headpiece with a long plastic visor pulled down over the front to protect her face.

"Sorry, you're not allowed inside. Insurance," she said. There was that word again. "But I can still use your help. Bring me the broom, a dustpan, and the trash can," she pointed.

I was tired of thinking about bonking animals so I was happy to get moving and focus on helping her clean. We worked together on each of the three enclosures. She said the eagles scared her the most. "My head and face are protected, but not my arms," she told me. Again, I admired her bravery, and again, I thought. . . I could never be a zookeeper.

She told me, "The raptors need to be fed before the park opens. . ." and then she paused, and I thought she would add "for obvious reasons" but I guess it was so obvious she didn't feel the need to say it.

* * *

Our cart was still loaded with trash barrels and birdseed when we'd finished with the raptors. Lisa drove us over to the fencing that surrounded the pond that was the center of the zoo. She asked me to hop out when we approached the gate and handed me a set of keys with the one I needed pointing up. I unlocked the gate padlock, pushed it open wide, and proceeded to close it behind her as she drove the cart through.

She hopped out of the cart and turned to me excitedly, "Today, we're going to check nesting boxes!" I didn't know if her happiness was for me or if she was as glad to be done with raptor feeding as I was. I grabbed a trash can and a bucket of seed and followed her.

"We'll rake first, then lay seed, and then we get to check the nesting boxes," she explained. I was curious about what checking nesting boxes entailed, but I was done asking questions for the moment.

She directed me to a ground area with lots of bird droppings, and I headed that way with a rake in hand. I was getting a quick education in the varying sizes of bird poop.

The pond was beautiful and full of every kind of waterfowl you could imagine: mallards, coots, swans, Canada geese, green-winged teals, and the most beautiful duck I'd ever seen, which I learned was called a wood duck. I thought they looked like hand-painted artwork. It was hard to believe they were real until you watched them gliding across the water. They were a bit more skittish than the mallards. Most of the birds swarmed the shore to greet Lisa, who followed behind me as I raked. She spread seeds and cracked corn. No one had to die to feed the ducks.

I noticed that these birds could leave the pond at any time, and there was an inlet of water that came right up to the zoo's property not fifty yards away, so I supposed they did sometimes leave, but they must always come back. Who can pass up a sure thing like a daily free meal? The juxtaposition of these free waterfowl enjoying water, food, sun, and freedom next to the raptors locked in bird cages with roofs that blocked the sky wasn't lost on me. Thinking about it hurt.

"Okay, follow me, I need your help with the boat," she gave me a sly grin.

"What boat?" I asked, grinning back.

"You'll see," she teased. So that's what all her excitement over checking nesting boxes was about.

Together we flipped over a rowboat and pulled it over to the shoreline of the pond, then she directed me to get in. "I have on boots, you don't," she explained. "And you might want to invest in some," she looked at my tennis shoes like they weren't up to the task, and as the day progressed, I would have to agree.

I climbed into the wobbly boat, hoping I wouldn't fall into the water. I'm pretty clumsy. I've been told I like to set things in mid-air and expect them to stay there. Some part of me just didn't seem to have a handle on the physical world. Please don't let me tip us over! I prayed to myself as I tried to fold my long legs into the boat.

Lisa stepped into the water with her very appropriate boots and gave us a little push while hopping in at the same time. I admired her graceful coordination, which was something I sorely lacked.

She pulled a clipboard out and faced toward me, "This is where we chart nest activity."

I glanced over and saw a grid of box numbers and columns, some with checkmarks, some with egg counts, and some just blank.

In all my visits to the zoo, I had never noticed the nesting boxes. They were all around the outer rim of an island that stood in the middle of the pond. Each box had a number painted on it. Some of the boxes were well hidden by shrubbery. The island itself was full of vegetation and teeming with waterfowl.

We approached the first box. "We need to be very slow and quiet so we don't startle the occupants," she said as she carefully and slowly lifted the lid of the box. I held my breath waiting for a bird to fly out, like a wound-up jack-in-the-box, but nothing happened. No bird, but there sat three beautiful eggs, and Lisa checked her chart, made a note, and we moved on. "Those were there last week," she remarked.

We proceeded around the island in this fashion for the next thirty minutes or so. Sometimes surprising birds, who then surprised us in an escaping flurry of feathers; other times we found empty boxes or a clutch of eggs. Whatever we found was dutifully recorded by Lisa.

* * *

It was 10 a.m., and the park was opening, time for our first break. I was dying for a cigarette but didn't want to mention it. I was wondering if I would have an opportunity to smoke when Lisa pulled a pack of cigarettes out of her pants pocket and asked, "Mind if I smoke?"

I was so relieved, I almost laughed. "Mind if I join you?"

"Of course!" she said, and she offered me one of hers, but like a typical smoker, I carried my own. We drove our cart back toward the kitchen, puffing away on our respective cigarettes.

To the left of the kitchen was a large gate that led to a staff area not accessible to the public. Lisa handed me a set of keys and asked me to open the gate, so I hopped out and did as she requested.

As soon as she drove through, I shut and locked the gate and walked over to where she had parked. I couldn't help but glance at the back of the kitchen. Sure enough, it was there, right by the door. The drowning trap Lisa had told me about while we cleaned and fed raptors. My body shuddered.

"I hope you brought a snack," the sound of Lisa's voice distracted me from my morbid thoughts. "If not, the cafe should be open now." I didn't have anything with me, but I wanted to finish my cigarette anyway.

She said, "See you in fifteen!" and moved toward the kitchen.

I sat on a giant tree stump that was at least three feet wide, smoking and trying not to look at the drowning trap. I watched as keepers and volunteers all began to gather outside or proceed into the kitchen. Many were smoking. This was the 1980s. Almost everybody smoked.

I saw the keeper who had let me in the gate that morning and gave him a little wave and a smile. To my surprise, he walked over.

"Hi, I'm Matt," he put his hand out for a shake.

I moved my cigarette to my left hand and shook his with my right. "I'm Jeanie."

"How's your first day going?" he asked.

"I'm lovin' it," I had to shade my eyes when looking at him as the sun was just behind his head.

"What string are you on?" he asked.

"Five," I answered.

"All the volunteers want to start with monkeys . . ." he mockingly complained. "Maybe you'll help me out with elephants someday?" he asked with a cocky smile.

"Sure, I'd love to," I said, feeling a bit like a traitor to both Lisa, whom I had promised to work with on Saturdays, and my boyfriend, Brad. We had been having relationship problems, and Matt felt like the possibility of something new.

Sea Lions vs. Seals

Animals are so easily overlooked, their
interests so easily brushed aside.
— Matthew Scully

After a snack of peanut butter crackers and a Pepsi from the cafe, I met up with Lisa behind the kitchen.

"We need to get some fish together for No Name," she informed me.

"No name?" I asked.

"Yes, the sea lion. That's his name," she grinned.

"Is this a comedy routine?" I joked. "Like 'Who's on first?'"

She laughed, "I know it's strange, but somehow he never got a name, and so No Name stuck. You'll get used to it. Let's head over to the freezer."

Lisa carried an empty bucket and proceeded to a second walk-in located to the left of the refrigerator walk-in. Here we had more shelves full of food, and she walked over to the one designated for fish. "We'll take fish from this freezer and leave it in the refrigerator to thaw," she said as she pulled frozen fish into her bucket.

Once it was full, we walked together to the walk-in right next door. "That's one of yesterday's buckets," she pointed. "Pull that down, and I'll put this one in its place," she directed me to one of two buckets sitting side-by-side on the shelf. "No Name has two feedings a day, so whenever I take a bucket of thawed fish, I replenish it with a bucket of frozen ones," she explained.

I grabbed the bucket and walked with her back to the kitchen. She placed some of the fish onto the island. "We supplement his fish diet with protein powder and I need to add medicine and vitamins, so first I'll open a few fish and stuff them with a little of each."

I watched as she placed some pills inside the slit bellies of two fish and split the protein powder into two others, then placed these four on top of the fish that were left in the bucket. "I'll give him these four first to ensure he gets what he needs," she explained. Then she kind of laughed, "Not that there'll be any leftovers, he's a good eater."

I felt so grateful to Lisa for all of the information she imparted. She treated me as an equal and as if she were training me for her position. I'd find out later that not all keepers were teachers like Lisa. Some hardly talked at all.

Once again, we headed to our cart. We dumped the trash cans into an industrial-sized dumpster near the employee entrance gate. I could see why the gate was big enough for a vehicle as I assumed one had to drive through it to occasionally empty the dumpster. We placed our empty cans back on the cart along with the bucket of fish and our rakes and brooms, then off we drove.

Before Lisa could get the sea lion's gate open, No Name started barking. It was the funniest sound, like a dog but not like a dog, and it just made me happy to hear it. Was he happy too? I hoped so.

Lisa asked me to stay back while she proceeded into the pool area. I watched from the sidelines as she worked No Name into a routine for the audience of zoo-goers that had gathered in front of his pool. There had been multiple announcements about the sea lion feeding time, and this was the "morning show." I had an up-close and personal view of it from inside the gate, which made me feel privileged and lucky all at the same time.

With a gesture, Lisa asked No Name to circle the pool. He jumped into the water, swam a quick lap, then jumped back out again just as she tossed him the first fish, which he caught with ease. As she put him through some other routines, the crowd applauded, and I watched from my close viewpoint with amazement. I wondered how she learned to work with him. She had him bump her fist and kiss her cheek, hit a beach ball, project his body through a loop, and wave to the crowd. Each time he did as she asked, he was rewarded with a fish.

After his feeding show, the crowd slowly moved away. Some of them wandered over to the raptors, and I couldn't help remembering their feeding time earlier that morning. I wondered if any animal parts were visible at the bottoms of their cages. My thoughts turned back to the task at hand as Lisa and I proceeded to clean the area around the pool. No Name was penned in the back, mostly for my safety.

"Had you ever worked with seals before?" I asked curiously.

"No Name is a sea lion, not a seal," she explained. "A lot of people confuse them, but the way he barks, that's a sea lion trait. Seals just make soft grunts. And did you notice how he can sit up on his front flippers and wave? Seals lay mostly on their bellies and their flippers aren't that large."

"I had no idea they were different animals," I said.

She continued, "A quick way to tell if you're looking at a seal or a sea lion is that sea lions are brown and their ear flaps stick out," she flicked her own ears.

"How did he learn to do those things?" I asked. "Did you teach him?"

"He knew all of that when I got here. I'm the one who had to learn his routine, but I am trying to teach him new things," she perked up. "The crowd loves it."

"His pool's kind of small though," I commented cautiously, not knowing how she would take it. I was staring over at the oval of water that resembled a small backyard pool, only his was all deep end with no shallow area. It did have a few steps leading up to a platform where Lisa stood for his show.

"I suppose. . ." she paused. "I wanted him to have a companion, but they said a male sea lion needs more than one female and the space is too small. The zoo's trying to get accredited so they've been slowly doing away with the smaller enclosures and trying to set everything up to meet the standards of the Association of Zoos and Aquariums (AZA)."

I was glad they were trying to meet the standards of accreditation, but I wished No Name wasn't alone. I guessed it was better than having more sea lions in such a small space.

"Do you remember the chimpanzees that used to be here?" she asked me.

"Yes, but I haven't seen them for a while," I replied.

"I understand they had to relocate them because their living environment didn't meet the accreditation standards," she told me.

"You know, I always felt bad for them. . . they

didn't seem happy at all," I said, and she nodded in agreement. "I remember from my childhood that the male would spit at people," I added.

Their iron-barred cage was a small square compared to their size. They could get from one end to the other in just a few movements. They spent most of their time just sitting there. I noticed the door to their indoor home would often be closed, forcing them to be on display. Some zoo-goers would tease them or throw food at them. More than once, I saw the male eating a lollipop. There were signs asking visitors not to feed the animals, of course, but the zoo staff couldn't always be there to stop the rule-breakers, and I guess they weren't able to take the candy away once he had it. Would you take a lollipop from a male chimpanzee? I'm not sure you could if you tried. They are supposed to be as strong as four humans.

I was relieved when they were gone. Their presence made me uncomfortable. I didn't take time to examine my feelings about it when I was a child. Instinctively, I knew how wrong it was to keep such incredible creatures locked in a cage. My gut didn't like it, so out-of-sight and out-of-mind felt better. I remembered there was nothing natural about their enclosure either. No access to grass or leaves or even a bit of dirt. There was concrete flooring and there were iron bars. The only extra enrichment they had was a tire swing. The more I learned about chimpanzees and their needs—both socially and in their habitats—the more I would look back on their time at the zoo as torture. I hoped they found something better, wherever they ended up.

Lisa interrupted my thoughts with a surprising question. "Did you know they once escaped from the zoo and had to be captured by the police?"

"You're kidding?" My jaw dropped. How had I never heard about this?

"I am not kidding! Chuck, that was the male's name, they think he was the instigator. Judy, the female, ended up in someone's garage. They were both safely returned, though I doubt they were happy to be back."

"I wonder what their new home is like," I said wistfully.

"I hear they went to a sanctuary in Texas," she answered.

"Well, that's good, right?" I asked.

"Yes, that is good indeed."

* * *

At lunchtime, I was pretty much on my own. I could have hung out in the kitchen, but I felt a bit intimidated by all of the zookeepers, especially the head keeper, Monica, who kept a radio on her hip — as did all the keepers — barking orders to her staff and sending people to different strings when help was needed. When I first started volunteering, I thought Monica disliked me, but with time, I realized it wasn't personal. She didn't seem to like anybody. It was just her nature. At any rate, she was in the kitchen, eating her frozen dinner — veal parmesan, I heard her tell someone — and I wasn't comfortable enough to join them. Besides, it was a beautiful day at the zoo, perfect for eating outside.

I went to the cafe and picked up a tuna sandwich — I would eventually become vegetarian, and then vegan, but at this time I mostly ate "seafood." I took my lunch with me to a bench in the barnyard area. I loved this section of the zoo most when it wasn't lunchtime and buzzing with zoo-goers and screaming children, but it was nice to hang out near the petting zoo animals and watch the pigeons and guinea hens roam freely through the area looking for handouts. Sometimes I'd see peacocks, too. Unlike the pigeons, they kept to themselves, but I could admire their beauty and their piercing calls from afar. If I sat in the sun with my eyes closed and listened to them, I felt like I'd been transported to a jungle.

* * *

After lunch, Lisa took me to the docent building located behind the kitchen. Lisa explained that the docent animals were used for educational purposes. Specially trained volunteers, called docents, would take animals from the building out to the public areas of the zoo as well as off the zoo property to schools and events. They would then hold live animal presentations and talk about the animals and their purpose at the zoo.

Lisa took me around to each cage to introduce me to the animals inside. This small building that was tucked out of sight of the public eye held chinchillas, snakes, rabbits, lizards, and just one tarantula. We would clean their cages, prepare their food, and freshen their water.

Of all the animals in that building, I enjoyed the chinchillas the most. Those tiny little creatures had the softest fur I'd ever felt. And their big eyes, huge ears, and timid nature made them all the more endearing to me. I asked Lisa, "Are these the animals they make into fur coats?"

"Yes, can you imagine how many of them it must take to make one coat?" she asked emphatically.

I looked at the tiny animals, sitting on their fake tree limbs, "Do they get any bigger?" I asked.

She shook her head, "No."

"Even killing one would be wrong," I continued.

She nodded in agreement, "True, but it takes a lot more than one to make a fur coat. Try two hundred," she said with disgust.

"Good Lord!" I exclaimed.

I learned that chinchillas are from the Andes mountains in South America where some were captured and brought to the United States to be bred as pets, for use in laboratories, or for their fur. In the wild, they would live in groups, dig burrows, and tuck themselves into rock crevices for protection from the elements.

I think my proudest moment in that building was the first time I held a snake. I surprised myself by readily picking up the small one. I needed to move them to temporary containers while I cleaned their cages. I almost flinched when the first one wiggled, but I suppressed the feeling for fear that I would drop him. I wanted Lisa to view me as capable, but more importantly, I didn't want to harm them. The snakes weren't poisonous so there was really no reason to be afraid of them, but that never stopped my fear of cockroaches. I found snakes to be surprisingly soft and smooth, and not at all slimy, which was what I had expected.

The one creature that I hoped to avoid was the tarantula. Lisa teased me and said, "Think of it as a small kitten, all furry and cute."

"Yeah, not likely," I laughed.

As she cleaned his tank, I noticed she never

actually handled the spider; she just used a series of maneuvers with the lid to move him from one side of his home to the other while she cleaned what little there was to clean. I realized I could do that, and from that point forward, I did.

"What does he eat?" I asked.

"We feed him crickets mostly," she said. And that reminded me of all the animals at the zoo who ate other animals at the zoo.

Like the other docent animals, the tarantula had just a tiny bit of space, but more disturbing was that he was alone.

* * *

I left the zoo at 3 o'clock on that first Saturday. I smoked like a chimney on the drive home with the window halfway down and a cool breeze flowing into my jalopy of a car. I couldn't wait to tell my sister, Zoey, all about what I had learned and experienced. Zoey and I were just two years apart and shared a home with a roommate friend.

When I walked into the door, my cat, Ginger, came running up to me. She reminded me of a dog with her persistent sniffing. I couldn't imagine what she was thinking about all the smells I'd brought home with me. I was filthy from head to toe, and my tennis shoes were pretty much done for. I was already pondering how I could afford to buy the boots that Lisa recommended. More than anything, I wanted a shower!

I saw Zoey when I reached the living room, and she laughed at the sight of me. "Don't you look like something the cat dragged in?" she said.

"Yes, literally!" I pointed to Ginger at my feet, and

we laughed. "And I feel like it, too," I said. "I have sore muscles where I didn't know I had muscles!"

"So, how was it?" she asked.

"Wonderful," I smiled. "Amazing and . . . and eye-opening. You wouldn't believe what really goes on behind the scenes at the zoo!"

"Really? Like what?" she asked.

"Well, for one thing, I'm glad I didn't choose the exhibit building. Lisa, the keeper I worked with today, told me that they have so many roaches in the back area of that building that they fall off the ceiling and onto your head!"

Zoey grimaced, and said, "Oh my God, that would freak me out!"

"I know," I laughed. "And cockroaches at the zoo are huge, not like your typical house roach." I told her about fire-hosing the giant cockroach in monkey house, and we laughed together.

"Oh, and by the way, I'm in love. . ." I batted my eyelashes and grinned at the look on her face. "Let me finish…" I paused, ". . . with a monkey," I said with a laugh.

"Oh," she laughed too. "I was wondering. . ."

"His name is Monkers, and he's my age," I smiled, "and he likes to have his belly scratched."

'I'm so happy for you, Jeanie," she said.

And then I said, "But seriously, there was this cute guy…"

"Uh-oh, did you and Brad break up . . . again?" she rolled her eyes.

"Not yet," I laughed.

* * *

That night, I headed over to Brad's. We had

recently gotten back together after a three-month stint apart in which we'd both dated other people.

I let myself into his apartment and found him at his keyboard where he spent most of his free time.

"So, how was it?" he asked.

"I loved it, and I can't wait to go back," I told him.

"You know Jeremy worked there years ago," he said. Jeremy was Brad's oldest brother. I had forgotten all about that, and I was surprised we hadn't talked about it when I started planning to volunteer, but then I remembered that we hadn't seen much of each other in the last few months.

"Oh right, I forgot all about that," I replied.

"They let him take a monkey home with him for a while," he said.

"Wow, I just learned about that today, keepers can help raise baby monkeys if they need to… I worked with the monkeys today," I said.

We talked more about my day and decided to head out to a seafood restaurant for dinner.

After dinner and back at his apartment, I was full and tired. I had gotten up earlier than usual and been more physically active than I'd been in a very long time. Once I had a full belly, it was all I could do to keep my eyes open. Brad had pulled the hide-a-bed out, and I was sitting on the mattress doing crosswords while he played at the piano when the phone rang.

It was Elaine, the woman Brad had dated when we split up. I had a bad feeling about this. It was the third time she'd called him, that I knew of, since we'd gotten back together, and he always acted so cagey about her. He talked to her in that weird sing-song voice, like he was trying to let her know that he wasn't alone.

When he hung up the phone, he went back to

playing music as if it was no big deal, but I couldn't shake my instincts and blurted out to him, "She's pregnant, isn't she?"

He blanched, and his face went white.

"How did you know?" he asked.

"Oh my God, she is?" I asked incredulously. "Brad, how could you be so careless after what we went through? We would have had a child together. Us." I was young, only seventeen when it happened. We'd been together about six months, and I was still in high school. We made the decision together not to continue the pregnancy, and now the thought of another woman having his child when he and I were the ones who were supposed to be in love and together was making me ill. I felt helpless.

"I don't know what to say…" He paused. "It was an accident, you know," he said.

"Didn't you use birth control?!" I asked angrily. I thought to myself, it's one thing to be young and stupid, but another thing entirely to be almost 30 years old and still making this kind of mistake.

"She said she couldn't get pregnant!" he was almost yelling. "She's never used birth control before and has never gotten pregnant," he said.

I rolled my eyes, "Are you kidding me?" How naive could he be? "I don't know if I can handle this," I said, nearing tears.

"I know," his shoulders slumped, defeated.

"What's she going to do?" I wanted to know. I needed to know.

"I don't know," he shook his head. "But I love YOU," he stared at me steadily, unblinking.

I loved him too, but I didn't know if it was enough.

We didn't talk about it anymore that night. I had to get some sleep, and there was nothing else to say. The situation was putting a huge strain on our already strained relationship. I wasn't sure there was a future for us.

* * *

On Sunday, I got up early, and after making a quick stop at my house to feed Ginger and change my clothes, I went out to my mom's house. I loved spending Sundays at my mom's. We would play cards while we talked, eat lots of food, and smoke cigarettes together. My mom and step-dad lived in a trailer having semi-retired, meaning he was retired but she continued to work retail jobs because she not only wanted but needed her own money — mostly to support her tobacco habit. She smoked three packs of cigarettes a day.

After greeting each other with a hug, we sat at the kitchen table and started a game of cards while we talked about my day at the zoo, from scratching Monkers' belly to handling a snake.

"You better be careful," she said.

"Don't worry mom, they're not poisonous," I assured her.

"I'm not talking about the snakes, I'm talking about the monkeys! They can be mean. And they bite!" she stated emphatically.

"Oh mom," I rolled my eyes and laughed but assured her that I was perfectly safe.

* * *

The next few months flew by. Though Brad and I were continuing our relationship, we no longer seemed fully committed. I could feel us moving away from each other, and I thought the next breakup we had would likely be the last. The tension between us was thick.

I was a regular zoo volunteer now, arriving every Saturday morning promptly at 7 o'clock. My work with Lisa became routine. She began to give me more and more tasks that I could complete without her assistance. I could take care of cleaning monkey house and preparing their food without her looking over my shoulder and then we'd meet up to do their yards together. I started to feel more like a fellow zookeeper and less like a volunteer with each passing week. What I didn't know was that I soon would be moving to another string.

On what would turn out to be one of my last regular days on String 5, I was standing with Lisa as she gave a presentation on spider monkeys to the public. Rosie had birthed a baby boy and the zoo staff had named him Billy Bob. He was now a major zoo attraction. With reports on the TV news and in the local paper, people were flocking to the zoo to see the new arrival. There are not many things cuter than a baby spider monkey.

Before Lisa started her presentation, she handed Billy Bob to me to hold. She began talking about his birth and the precautions the zoo staff had to take in case the mother didn't respond in a nurturing way. All their preparation turned out to be unnecessary as Rosie took to motherhood like a fish to water, and all the other monkeys in her troop accepted Billy Bob as well.

Billy Bob was a squirmy little thing, and I found holding him to be a challenge. Before Lisa could finish her presentation, he bit me, and I let out a loud yelp. Lisa, who'd been looking out at the crowd, hadn't seen what happened, but heard the audience's nervous laughter, because Billy Bob had not just bitten me anywhere, he had latched onto my right boob. I was able to quickly push him off but not before most everyone had noticed. Everyone but Lisa, who looked at me with confusion, then scooped him out of my arms and completed the rest of her talk. I stood by awkwardly, no longer having a purpose at her demonstration except embarrassment.

As soon as we got back into monkey house, I explained to Lisa what had happened, and she burst out laughing.

I couldn't wait to tell my mom that she was right. Monkeys do bite.

The Barnyard

All animals are equal, but some animals
are more equal than others.
— George Orwell, *Animal Farm*

I had missed several weekends at the zoo. Brad and I had broken up. I knew it was coming, had expected it — heck, I even helped it along. Yet it still managed to come as a surprise. I decided staying at home was the last thing I should be doing. I started going out with friends on Friday nights, so I missed a lot of Saturdays. I finally switched my volunteer days to Sundays.

More than ever, I needed my weekends at the zoo. It felt like an escape from the real world, and the work was so satisfying. I got to hang out with animals, do something physical, and complete tasks over and over again. Quite the opposite of my office job, which was mostly sitting, typing, and talking on the phone. I sometimes considered applying for a zookeeper job, but then I would remind myself of the unimaginable tasks that would be required of me. Bonking animals to be fed to other animals and dealing with cockroaches falling from the ceiling of the EB. I knew from my conversations with Lisa that the keepers worked wherever they were needed. Unlike volunteers, they couldn't avoid any tasks. If I was a zookeeper, I would not be at liberty to choose my work.

Unfortunately, Lisa didn't work on Sundays, and

they already had a regular volunteer on String 5, so they asked me to work String 1, which included the barnyard animals. As long as it wasn't the Exhibit Building (where the cockroaches roam), I was happy to do it.

Working with domestic animals was relatively stress-free. For one thing, they were herbivores so there were no body parts to deal with at feeding time. There was also no chance of a raptor attacking the keeper and no tarantula to maneuver around. All the same, I missed Lisa and my regular string favorites like Billy Bob and Monkers, who still grunted softly and pressed his belly against the fence every time he saw me.

On this first Sunday, I was working with a tall blond, sturdy-looking woman named Sherry. Sherry didn't work Saturdays so we had never met. She took me to the barn to start. I'd been to the barn on many occasions as a zoo visitor, and I loved the smell of it. The hay, the animals, even the manure. The odors took me back to my teen years when I used to ride horses with one of my best friends, Karen. Karen had worked out a deal with a man who boarded horses in our neighborhood. If we cleaned his horse stalls, he'd let us ride his horse, Frosty. We'd get up at 5:30 in the morning on some weekends so we could spend the day on Frosty after mucking stables to earn our privileges. Karen knew all about horses and rode them in shows. She'd also taken me to more than one rodeo, but I eventually became too uncomfortable with the violence. The animals were forced into fearful and harmful situations and it just didn't sit well with me. I started to feel like an outsider for not enjoying the events so I just avoided them altogether.

Sherry's voice brought me back to the present, "We need to clean all the indoor stalls before moving to the outdoor yards. Clear everything from the floors — waste, hay, everything. We'll scrub them down and rinse them with the hose before we let the animals back in," she explained. This was pretty much the same routine as monkey house, just a different environment.

The floors were made of cement so it was fairly easy to clear them — a lot easier than my horse barn cleaning days. I enjoyed going to each stall, clearing and cleaning, and moving to the next one. It gave me a nice feeling of accomplishment, and I got to visit with the animals who were sunbathing on the other side of their half doors.

The barn housed two donkeys, two sheep, a cow and her almost full-grown calf (who was getting big enough to have his own stall), four goats, and two gigantic pigs named Laverne and Shirley. There were also birds on the outside of the barn in neighboring enclosures. There were two junglefowl that looked like exotic and colorful chickens from the tropics, and maybe they were. A male and female turkey also shared a pen. In the back of the barn was a drawer full of eggs that were being incubated. Someday soon, they would be hatching into baby chicks. A difficult reminder of their fate.

Once the stalls were cleared, scrubbed, and hosed, we used a squeegee to get the water off the floors before we added a fresh layer of hay. We then filled their feeders and let the animals back inside. Like the monkeys, they returned indoors with ease knowing food awaited them.

While they were eating indoors, we raked and cleaned their outdoor stalls, and then opened their half doors so they could move in and out as they pleased. Zoo-goers could see them either way by coming into the public area inside the barn or walking up to the fencing surrounding their outdoor stalls.

After the barn's indoor and outdoor stalls were cleaned, we moved to the barnyard. This area was known as the petting zoo. People were allowed to touch and feed the animals, so long as the food came from one of several feeders attached to the fence. You could insert a couple of quarters and get a handful of grain. However, unlike most "petting zoos," visitors were not allowed inside with the animals so this was my first time within the fenced barnyard. And this was the first time, other than the duck pond, that I'd actually been tasked with cleaning an area while the animals were still in it. All the other times, the animals were transferred back and forth so that whatever yard, stall, or cage I was cleaning was empty at the time.

We moved some of the stable animals with us to the yard, including Marmalade, the mama cow, and her son, Rocky. Rocky was quite beautiful, with velvet-looking fur and large doe-like eyes brimming with thick, long eyelashes. He liked to follow me around and his attention made me nervous—he was young, but large and rambunctious. Most of the time he just wanted a little scratch behind the ears or around his short horns. I would rake a little, pet Rocky, and rake again. He never seemed to get enough. I'd give him a few scratches and move on, only to have him follow me some more. Rocky was one of the reasons I would eventually stop eating hamburgers. When you have a loveable lug like him following you around like a puppy, it's kind of hard to imagine eating him.

By the time we'd finished the barnyard, visitors were arriving. The zoo was open and it was time for our first break. I found my favorite tree stump behind the kitchen and smoked a cigarette alone. Sherry wasn't a smoker and had gone into the kitchen, presumably for a snack or a chat with her fellow keepers.

Our next task was to take care of the smaller domestic animals on our string. These were a combination of guinea pigs and rabbits as well as the larger docents, and they weren't seen by the public but were kept in the area behind the kitchen and the building referred to as EB.

Sherry tasked me with cleaning the animal hutches while she worked in the small fenced-in grazing yard that was currently home to two llamas who were used as docent animals.

Handling the guinea pigs and rabbits was bittersweet because I knew that at least some of them would end up as food for other zoo animals. I'd stare into their adorable little faces, and gently handle their furry little bodies as I moved them into transfer bins in order to clean their homes, and my heart would break with the secret knowledge of their future. I envied other volunteers who hadn't been exposed to the true purpose of their short lives here behind the zoo.

Sun Bears and Bison

In nature, nothing is perfect and
everything is perfect.
— Alice Walker

Before lunch, we prepared a small pick-up truck for our next ventures to the sun bears and American bison. In the same rear area of the zoo, behind the kitchen and to the left of the walk-ins, there was a hay barn. Hay was delivered on a regular basis and stacked to the ceiling inside. Sherry and I donned sturdy gloves and grabbed about a half dozen bales of hay, loading them into the truck bed along with our tools of the trade—trash cans, rakes, and shovels.

Our first stop was just past the barnyard and toward the zoo's entrance. The Malaysian sun bears are the smallest of the world's eight bear species. We had pulled together their diet of fruit, vegetables, and kibble. Once the connecting doors were closed between their indoor and outdoor areas, we made our way inside to begin cleaning.

As we cleaned I remarked to Sherry, "I don't usually visit the sun bears, I feel kind of sorry for them because their exhibit is so small."

Sherry paused before replying, "I suppose it is a bit small. In the wild they sit up in the trees—I'm not sure how we could offer them that here. . ."

"Wow, I didn't realize they lived in trees. They sure don't have anything like that here," I said as I looked around their cement structure.

After cleaning, we left food inside and opened their doors. They came sauntering in. They looked so awkward and clumsy on the ground with really long claws that Sherry pointed out to me. "That's one of the reasons they can climb trees," she gestured. "And the crescent on their chest? That's how they got their name."

The crescent she referred to was a half-circle of lighter-colored fur. They really were unique-looking creatures.

* * *

When the sun bears were cleaned and fed, we drove across a large span of the walkway to the land of the American bison. They were out in their yard when we arrived. Sherry quickly pulled on a rope to shut their entrance into the barn. She then asked me to count the animals. It took me some rubber-necking to find them all, but I came up with the number she was looking for, five. Sherry explained to me that, unlike the farm animals, we were not allowed in the same enclosures as the bison under any circumstances. Bison are about six feet tall, can weigh up to a ton, and can run up to 30 miles per hour. For that reason, we were always to ensure that we counted the animals when we transferred them back and forth from their yard to their barn.

Only after the bison count in the yard was confirmed could we then open our side of the barn. Even though I knew they were all outside, having just heard all of the stats on bison, I felt nervous when we first opened the door; but of course, we found the barn empty.

Bison manure was the heaviest I'd dealt with, and there was a lot of it. We pulled in a trash can and began the process of shoveling up the contents of the open stall floors of the barn. It was summer, and the heat of the barn mixed with the smell of manure, made the stench even more pronounced. My arm muscles were sore from lifting shovelfuls into trash cans, and sweat was dripping into my eyes. It was a grueling task.

Once the barn was clean, we grabbed half of the hay bales from the truck and carted them inside. Sherry used a knife to cut the bands that held the bales together, and we each took stacks to the bisons' feed bins. Sherry also provided them with a supplemental food called herbivore pellets. Now that all of the cleaning and food prep was complete, we just needed to transfer the animals into the barn so that we could clean their outdoor area. First, we left the barn and secured the door on our side, then Sherry pulled on a second rope to re-open the barn door on their side. Once the door was open, she yelled for them and banged on the side of a food can.

In bison herds, the females—called "cows"—are the leaders. In this herd, the leader was the oldest female, and her name was Diana, which I at first thought was a silly name for a bison, but then again, Diana in mythology was the goddess of wild animals, so I decided it was a pretty respectable name after all. Diana trotted toward the barn ahead of her companions, and they all dutifully followed. It was an uncanny sight to see them running toward us and then into the barn. They were so big and so beautiful, and they reminded me of Native Americans and the wild west.

Once we thought they were all in the barn, Sherry turned to me, "Before we enter their yard, we need to make sure they're all out of it."

I turned to the yard to view it but Sherry explained, "No, we don't check by looking at the yard, we check by looking in the barn. It would be easy to miss one in the yard, and that's not a mistake you want to make. Don't rely on what you might not be able to see, always count what you can see!"

She walked to the barn window, and I followed. I silently counted each one as she counted them out loud. One - Two - Three - Four - Five. We shut them into the barn.

As we entered the gate to their yard and began walking past the barn, that was the first time I noticed just how big of an area they were housed in — their yard was huge. As a visitor to the zoo on prior occasions, I could barely see them over the hedges that lined their fence. Now that I was on the inside, I could see just how far back it went — almost to the approaching inlet of water. Considering that bison are grazers by nature, I was glad they had room to move around, but in spite of its size, they had pretty much picked their yard clean of all grasses. In the wild, bison are roamers — meaning they cover a lot of ground, grazing as they travel. Any area of a zoo would be too confining.

Sherry took her rake to the right while I went left, positioning myself under a copse of trees that provided relief from the summer sun. As I was raking, I was just thinking about what a beautiful day it was when Sherry shouted, "Hey Jeanie, find your exit!"

Startled, I turned and asked, "Find my what?"

"Whenever you're working with these kinds

of animals, you have to have a plan of escape. If something happens, and the barn door flies open, where are you going to go?" she stared at me with a stern look on her face.

I waited, hoping she would tell me.

"Look to the edge of the yard. Just before the hedges, there's a huge ditch and an electric fence," she pointed, and I turned to look and could see what I hadn't noticed before, electric fencing running the perimeter of the yard.

"Oh, I see it," I said.

"That fence keeps the bison back, but there's plenty of room under the bottom wire for a human to fit," she continued. "So stay alert and aware of your surroundings, and always know where the nearest ditch is located. If you see a bison, don't wait, just run," she said in a very serious tone. "Roll yourself under the wire and right into the ditch, and they won't be able to reach you there."

"Okay, I will." I paused, then asked, "Has that ever happened to you? Have the bison busted out of the barn?"

"No. . ." she said. "But there's always a first time," she returned to her task.

We worked side-by-side, and I felt like I was on hyper-alert waiting for a bison to bust out of the barn. I tried to relax and enjoy the beauty of the day, but I was aware that I'd just been schooled in taking these animals very seriously.

Once we'd finished raking and scooping poop, we went over to the small pick-up truck for the rest of the hay and began carting bales into the yard. We exited the yard and triple-checked that the gate was closed and locked, then Sherry walked to the left side of the barn and used the pull rope to open the yard-side of the barn door. Now the bison were free to roam.

Sir Crane

Hope is the thing with feathers
That perches in the soul . . .
— Emily Dickenson

After bison, came lunch. Since Sherry didn't smoke, I didn't want to smoke around her. The work was satisfying, but my day wasn't as companionable as a day spent with Lisa. Sherry wasn't just more serious, she was also less talkative.

In the afternoon, Sherry and I drove in a light truck to the area that housed animals from Australia, Africa, and the American West. They were all located in the same section of the zoo. Like String 5, much of String 1 seemed to be based on location— mainly two locations. The bison were on the same side of the zoo as the barnyard animals, while the "A-continent" animals (as I came to think of them) were in adjoining yards that were separated only by tall chain-link fences.

Our first stop was the American white-tailed deer. Here, as with the domestic farm animals, we were able to work in their yards while the animals were present. In the rear of the yard, shaded by trees, was an open shed-like structure where they could seek shelter from the rain, and where we could leave their food. The front of the yard was open, with no trees and not much grass. Deer droppings, referred to as "scat," were the size and shape of tiny pellets, making raking a difficult task on the hard flat ground. The pellet poop was small enough to fit in between rake tines and round enough to roll away when I tried to gather it into a pile. I found a broom on the ground was more effective. The deer were beautiful and a pleasure to watch. I wanted to reach out and pet them, but they were too timid. I supposed that even these deer, who were safe from hunters, instinctively held inside them the fear of man.

After the deer, came Australia. The emus were housed with the wallabies in a yard that was similar to the deer yard but much smaller with shaded housing toward the back. It struck me that both of these animals were smaller versions of their more well-known cousins, the ostrich and the kangaroo.

Emus are the second-largest birds after ostriches, but they are from Australia, while ostriches are native to Africa. Both of these large birds are called ratites, because their breast bones are flat, and they can't fly. The emus at the zoo were accustomed to humans and pretty much ignored me while I cleaned their yard alongside them.

The wallabies, on the other hand, were timid, and avoided me entirely, which was probably best since I pretty much wanted to hug them to death, they were just that adorable. They looked so much like kangaroos that many zoo visitors mistook them for their babies, called joeys. Both kangaroos and wallabies are marsupials, meaning they carry their young in a pouch. But these zoo wallabies didn't have any young to carry.

After the work "down under" and another break, Sherry said we were heading over to the "ungulates."

"What's an ungulate?" I asked curiously. I had never heard that term before.

"An ungulate is a hoofed mammal—in this case, the oryx, which is like an antelope," she explained.

For some reason, the oryx were always referred to as ungulates by the zoo staff, even though there were quite a lot of other zoo animals that I thought—by definition—would fall in this category, including the white-tailed deer and the zoo's one hippo.

The oryx have a very striking appearance. Their bodies looked sturdy and strong, with mostly tan fur except for the bold stripes of darker fur that seemed to outline their bodies as it ran along their backs, under their bellies, and up their chests. Their faces, too, were outlined in dark fur over white noses, chins, and eyes—sort of the opposite of a raccoon. Their most distinctive feature was their extremely long, spear-like horns. Because of these horns and their nature (and the ever-present matter of "insurance"), we were not allowed to be in the yard with them. We first had to transfer them to their interior barn, which we did with the enticement of food, as I had learned was usually the case when transferring animals at the zoo.

Once safely housed, Sherry and I carried in our trash cans and rakes and began our usual clean-up routine. This seemingly simple task was complicated by a curious and persistent crane. The Grey Crowned Crane of Africa (also called the African Crane) is not a shy bird. In fact, quite the opposite. This beautiful fella had dark gray and white feathers with accents of orange, but his most remarkable feature was the spiky crown of feathers on his head, a testament to his name. This particular crane seemed to be fascinated with me. He followed my every move and pecked at my heels and my back whenever he got the chance. My time in that enclosure felt like a deja vu of my work in the barnyard when I was followed by Rocky the calf. Both of these animals seemed to notice the "new" volunteer, and pursue me with curiosity. In the case of Sir Crane (as I came to call him), I'd rake, feel a peck, and turn toward the source. When I turned to face him, he'd stop and act as if he hadn't done anything at all. But as soon as I turned back to my task, he'd return to his—and apparently, pecking me was his task. This went on for several minutes: rake, peck, turn; rake, peck, turn—repeatedly, over and over again.

Sherry was as confused by his attention as I was, and asked me, "Are you wearing anything shiny?"

I looked down and inspected my outfit—jeans, volunteer polo, boots (no more tennis shoes for me), jacket. "No," I answered, "not that I can see . . ."

"Well, I've never seen him do that . . ." she frowned.

"Is there any place we can put him while I'm raking?" I asked.

"No, sorry . . . but he's really harmless," she replied and turned back to her own raking.

He sure didn't feel harmless. As much as I liked this quirky little bird, his pecks were sometimes painful and always a surprise—even though I knew they were coming! One thing was for sure, he kept me on my toes.

I hadn't had a peck in about five minutes and was beginning to think he'd lost interest in me when I turned to see my newfound friend jumping up and down and flapping his wings.

Sherry saw him too. "I think that's a mating dance!" she exclaimed, and I thought that was the first time I'd seen her excited about anything.

I laughed out loud, "What? Really?" I felt honored.

After a bit of "dancing" he suddenly stopped, and we went back to our cleaning.

Now raking without my friend, I was lost in thought and wondered why there was no Mrs. Crane to keep him company.

* * *

Our last animals for the day were the ostriches. There were four of them in such a remote part of the zoo that I wasn't sure how many visitors made their way over to them. Ostriches are tall—I mean really tall. They are usually over six feet and the males can grow to nine feet. Though they may seem like they are all legs and neck, they can weigh up to 300 pounds. Like a lot of birds, the males have more distinct colors while the coloring of the females is beneficial for blending into their surroundings. In this case, the males are mostly black with some white accent feathers while the females are grayish brown. Their long eyelashes make them appear almost like a caricature, but they're not as friendly as they look. Because of their nature, and their strength, we were required to transfer them to another enclosure before we could clean their yard.

Once we entered, I asked Sherry, "Do they really put their heads in the sand?"

Sherry laughed. "No, they don't, but they can lower their bodies to the ground when they're trying to hide from a predator, like a lion. And if they're cornered, they'll use their powerful legs to fight, or they might just run away—they can run 30 to 40 miles per hour." I imagined driving my car at residential neighborhood speed only to be passed by an ostrich.

* * *

After the ostriches, Sherry dismissed me for the day. I wandered around the zoo for a while visiting different animals and eventually made my way to the elephants. As I approached, I noticed a truck parked in the rear of the building. My heart skipped a beat. Now that I was single again, I often wondered about Matt, and I was hoping to run into him.

Mammal house was home to the two African elephants, Mary and Heidi, but also held one hippo, two white rhinos, and two tapirs. The building was shaped like a crescent moon—the inner half-circle was a wall of windows with views of the animals' indoor areas, and the larger outer rim of the moon offered the animals access to their yards.

As I approached from the rear, I was facing the windowed inner circle. I went to the center area—the largest section of windows—and could see Matt and another keeper inside with the elephants. I noticed that both of "the girls"—as they were called by the keepers—were chained by their legs to iron loops coming out of their floor. They made a swaying motion with their bodies that made the movement limited by the chain all that more noticeable. Matt turned toward the window, and I waved at him. He then motioned for me to approach the staff entrance.

As I started to walk toward the door to my right, I could see him walking on the inside to meet me. I waited outside the locked door for only a second before he opened it and waved me inside. This was my first time entering mammal house and the feeling was electrifying—mostly because of the sheer magnitude of the animals it housed, but also because Matt was holding the door open for me.

"After you," he said with a wink and a smile. So he's a flirt, I thought. I just hoped he wasn't married. In my experience, there were plenty of "interested" men out there, but they weren't always single. I had already noticed that he didn't wear a ring, but in his line of work, it wouldn't be safe to wear one.

I stepped inside an anteroom that was stacked floor-to-ceiling with bales of hay. My senses were assaulted by the odors of mammal house. The first thing I noticed was the smell of fresh hay, then another more pungent odor hit my nostrils, one I had never smelled before but that I would soon come to associate with elephants.

Matt directed me to follow him as we walked the pathway between the windows to our left and the barred enclosures to our right. The first room we walked through housed the Asian tapirs—black-and-white animals with bodies shaped like a large pig and a trunk-like snout (much shorter than an elephant's). Most people think of them as some kind of exotic pig, but their looks are deceiving since they are actually related to horses and rhinos. As we moved past the tapir room, we entered the hallway of the second room, and voila! The only thing that stood between me and two enormous, gorgeous African elephants was a wall of vertical bars widely spaced enough so that a human could pass between them, but narrow enough to keep the elephants inside.

As I stood there in awe, Matt turned to me and asked, "So, what do you think?"

"They're . . . amazing," I replied, and then I blushed at my lame answer. "I can't believe how big they are — I mean they look so much larger in person." I continued, feeling awestruck but ineptly able to communicate it.

Even though the "girls" were chained to the floor, Matt directed me to stay on my side of the bars as he rejoined his fellow keeper, Holly, who gave me a glance but otherwise ignored me. They were doling out food.

I leaned back onto the half wall just below the windows. My heart was pounding with the excitement of being so close to elephants. I was overwhelmed by their size and grandeur. I admired how the keepers seemed to move around them with ease, unafraid. I was struck by the bravery that's required to do their jobs. Both keepers had metal hooks hanging from their belt loops. I later learned that they're called bullhooks, and the keepers used them to control the elephants and give them instructions.

When Matt came within earshot, I asked, "Why are they chained?"

Matt responded, "We have to chain them at night for their safety, and at mealtimes to ensure they are eating their own food." I watched both of the elephants as they methodically picked up their food with their trunks and stuffed it into their mouths. Then Matt turned to me, "So, what do you think? Are you ready to come over to String 3?" he was smiling.

I was flattered. "Sure," I answered with a smile of my own. "Will I be able to wash the elephants?" I remembered Jan's experience and was hoping to have the same.

"Oh, we don't allow the volunteers to wash the elephants anymore," he replied. At first, I thought he was teasing me, but then I realized he was serious.

"Oh . . ." I frowned with disappointment.

"Do you know the volunteer Jan?" he asked.

"Yes . . ." I replied hesitantly, "Well, sort of, we've been in the kitchen together a few times."

"Heidi here . . ." Matt gestured to the elephant on the right, "tore the jacket right off her back," his voice sounded serious, but his grin told me something else. He was proud of Heidi.

"Oh no! She wasn't hurt, was she?" I truly felt concerned for her, particularly now that I was close enough to feel the sheer power emanating from the elephants.

"No," he laughed, "just surprised. But since then, no more volunteers. Insurance, you know."

"Yes, I've heard a lot about 'insurance,'" I gestured with air quotes.

I understood but still felt disappointed. Washing elephants is something I'd wanted to do since that first day when I heard about it from Jan. I always assumed it was in my future. I'd often see her on Saturdays—excited and soaked from having just come from mammal house. I briefly wondered if the jacket that had been torn off of her was the same Steelers jacket I'd seen her wearing on my first day. Well, at least she had an exciting story to tell! I'd have to ask her about it the next time I saw her.

"We're just closing up, if you want to wait a few minutes, I'll walk out with you," Matt said.

"Sure, that'd be great," I answered, and my heart gave a little leap in my chest. That sounded like an invitation of some sort, right?

As Matt and Holly started their closing procedures, I asked, "Is there anything I can do to help?"

Matt answered, "Yes, you can start bringing hay down to the rhinos."

I quickly went to the anteroom and grabbed a hay bale, not a pleasant task without gloves, but I managed to get the hay down to the rhinos, who were located just past the elephants. Matt joined me there and pulled out a knife, cutting the bands, and then separating pads to distribute between the two rhinos, who stood by attentively. I headed back to get more hay, and when I returned, Matt asked me to take it to the next room. In that last room was the zoo's sole hippo. I set the hay where he instructed, and when he finished with the rhinos, he came in and began separating pads for the hippo.

As we were walking out, Matt locked things up behind us, and we headed to the anteroom to make our exit. Holly had left ahead of us in the truck, so we walked together toward the zoo kitchen and staff gate.

"So how long have you been working at the zoo?" I asked curiously.

"About three years now. It's the greatest job on the planet," he turned to me with a huge smile on his face. He gave off the vibe of a very laid-back surfer dude, and that impression was supported by his shaggy hair and tanned skin.

"How do you like being a volunteer?" he asked.

"It's the greatest non-paying job on the planet," I returned his smile, and we both laughed.

And Then There Was One

In the practice of tolerance, one's enemy is
the best teacher.
— Dalai Lama

The next several months at the zoo went by quickly. Since I'd come in and worked a Sunday, I was now comfortable working either weekend day and alternated back and forth to fit my schedule. Now that I had experience on two strings and several months of volunteering under my belt, I often didn't know where I'd be working until I arrived.

There was nothing like the zoo in the fall. The crisp air, the beautiful leaf colors, the bluest of blue skies, and a temperature that made outdoor labor easy. I'd always had a soft spot for fall—it brings a feeling of nostalgia to my heart—and now I had one more reason to love it.

On one particular fall morning, I arrived promptly at 7 and was put on String 1. Sherry was absent, so Lisa was working her string that day. I hadn't worked with Lisa in a while, and we fell into an easy companionable day.

After the morning barnyard, a smoke break, and splitting up small domestics, we began prepping the truck for the bison yard. I was in the barn pulling down hay bales when Lisa suddenly stopped me. She turned to me solemnly, and said, "We don't need that many. Didn't you hear the news?"

She was staring at me so intently, so seriously, but I had no idea what she was talking about. My heart skipped. "What news?" I'm sure my face showed my concern and confusion.

"The bison," she swallowed hard. "They all died, except Diana."

I was shocked. "Oh my God, what?! Why? What happened?" I was stumbling over my words.

"Sid, the zoo vet. He knocked them down. They do that once in a while, you know, to take blood, run tests, make sure they're healthy? And . . ." she would have kept talking, but I interrupted.

"What do you mean 'knocked them down'?" I had never heard that term. It reminded me of when vets euthanize animals but that's called "putting them down." This didn't make any sense.

She slowed down to explain, "Once a year, Sid, the zoo vet, will tranquilize them so he can take their blood, clean their teeth — that sort of thing," she searched my face to make sure I was following what she was saying. "When they tranquilize animals, they call it knocking them down. Anyway, they usually just wake back up..." tears welled up in her eyes. "But not this time, the bastard," she fought her tears with anger. "I think he gave them too much tranquilizer. None of them would wake up!"

"Oh my God, I just can't believe it," I was stunned and thinking about all of those beautiful creatures.

Lisa continued, "They were able to revive Diana, but that's probably because she's the largest," she said.

"Oh, poor Diana," I was nearing tears myself. "What must she be thinking? She must be wondering what happened to her companions."

"She thinks she's lost from her herd," Lisa explained.

"Well that just breaks my heart," I voiced out loud what I was feeling.

"We've moved Rocky in with her for now. At least she has someone to keep her company," she told me.

We finished preparing the truck solemnly. The loss of the bison was made more obvious by the emptiness of our truckload.

Once we drove over, I could see Rocky and Diana grazing quietly together in the bison yard. They were an odd-looking pair, a young steer and an old bison. It might have been comical if it wasn't so sad. I had to fight back tears.

We quietly went through the motion of cleaning their barn, transferring them inside, and cleaning their yard. It was as if neither of us wanted to disturb their peace by interrupting the quiet. It was the shortest time I'd ever spent in the bison yard.

"Will the zoo get more bison?" I finally asked as we were packing up to leave.

"Probably," she rolled her eyes, "it's what they do," she sighed, and that was the first time I'd seen her express judgment against zoo policy.

"What will happen to the vet?" I assumed he was in big trouble, maybe he'd been fired.

"Nothing," she smirked. "It was considered an accident, a fluke. He'll still be the zoo's vet," she said with obvious disdain for him.

* * *

Because we only had thirty minutes for lunch, we usually ate at the zoo, but on this day, Lisa wanted to go out for a change. We walked over to the kitchen, and she yelled into the break room, "Does anyone want something from McDonald's?"

Matt spoke up, "I do, I'll come with you," and he got up to join us.

We walked out to Lisa's car, and Matt insisted that I sit up front. I was happy he had joined us, but his presence in the back seat made me nervous. Whenever he was around I felt self-conscious and tongue-tied.

As Lisa drove, she and Matt began to discuss what was on everybody's minds. She looked at him in the rearview mirror, "So what do you think about what happened?"

"It's bullshit," Matt said emphatically. "Sid killed them, and they aren't even holding him accountable."

"I agree," Lisa shook her head. "How can they continue to use him and act like nothing happened? I understand there are accidents but … you know his reputation, right?"

"Which one?" Matt smirked.

I stayed quiet feeling that if I reminded them of my presence they might stop their candid conversation. I wanted to know what they thought.

"I heard he's an exotic animal snob," she explained. "Maybe the bison aren't 'exotic' enough for him?" her voice was dripping with sarcasm.

"All I know is I wouldn't trust him with my dog," Matt said matter of factly.

The rest of our trip to McDonald's was unremarkable. I got a fish sandwich and fries and the smell made my stomach growl. My morning's physical work made me want to scarf down my food, but I restrained myself in front of Matt.

After lunch, Lisa and I headed over to the deer pen. I cleaned their yard while she worked in neighboring

Australia. There was one doe who seemed to be getting used to me, and I approached her slowly, hoping to have the chance to pet her. Moving as smoothly as possible, I made my way step-by-step over to her . . . ten feet away, then seven, then five, nonchalantly moving as if she wasn't my target of interest at all. Just as I was bringing my arm up to reach out for her, not two feet away, she spooked and ran off. She was so beautiful. Big eyes hooded by thick lashes and a brown nose surrounded by white fur. All the deer had those adorable white tails. I sighed, maybe next time.

After chasing rolling pellets of deer scat with a broom, I had the pleasure of cleaning the oryx pen, and once again was followed and pecked by Sir Crane. Lisa just laughed, even when I told her it wasn't funny.

Part Two: Mammal House

As you develop your awareness in nature,
you begin to see how we influence all life
and how all life influences us. A key and
critical feature for us to know.
— Tony Ten Fingers (Wanbli Nata'u)

Tale of Two Elephants

There is mystery behind that masked
gray visage, and ancient life force delicate
and mighty, awesome and enchanted
commanding the silence ordinarily
reserved for mountain peaks great fires
and the sea.
— Peter Matthiessen

Throughout the fall, I continued working as a sort of floater based on need—switching me back and forth between strings 1 and 5. I wasn't seeing much of my original string, though, because it always had more than enough volunteers. As Matt remarked when I first started, everyone loves monkeys. I had let Monica know that I wanted to try string 3, but apparently, everyone loved elephants too.

I arrived one morning to find that Lisa had left the zoo. I was sad to hear she had gone and wished I'd had the opportunity to tell her goodbye. I knew she had been devastated by what happened to the bison, and she had grown more and more disgruntled with the zoo's decision to keep Sid as their vet. I heard that she had gone to a zoo in Philadelphia, and I thought the animals there would be lucky to have her. I admired her independent nature, as she had once again picked up her life and moved to a new job in a new state. But I was sad for the spider monkeys because many of them—especially Monkers—had been so close to her. Perhaps they wondered where she had gone, and—like the matriarchal bison Diana, they too may have felt that they had lost a part of their family. I'm sure they missed her loving and familiar presence.

When winter arrived, the volume of volunteers at the zoo slowed to a trickle. Winter meant arriving at the zoo in the dark and working in the cold—not very appealing, even to the dedicated. But once I learned that they had less help, I felt even more obligated to show up. I didn't want to be a fair-weather volunteer.

The zoo felt different in the winter. The cold weather meant many of the animals spent most of their time indoors. But as luck would have it, String 3 needed a Sunday volunteer that winter, and I was more than happy to take the spot. Mammal house quickly became my favorite string.

* * *

It was my first day on String 3, and I was—to put it mildly—absolutely ecstatic. My tummy was full of butterflies as I approached the zoo gate and Matt walked over to let me in.

"Well look who made it to String 3," he said with a smile.

And all I could do was smile back. Smile a silly smile like a silly girl.

"Come on, you can help me set the truck up," he said as he led me past the giant dumpster.

String 3's truck was the largest vehicle at the zoo, with a hydraulic liftgate that Matt showed me how to operate. "First," he said, "we need ten trash cans and four buckets."

We grabbed the cans and stacked five of them together, then tilted them on their edge so we could roll them onto the truck's gate, then after lifting the gate, we rolled them onto the truck.

Next, we backed the truck up to the hay barn and stocked up. Hay was kept in the anteroom of mammal house but with all those large animals to consume it on a daily basis, it was in constant need of replenishment. The barn was chock full of hay bales and it was fun to climb up the mountain of hay to grab a bale from the top and toss it down.

After we loaded the truck with hay, Matt pulled a slip of paper off a clipboard he kept in the truck's cab.

"Gather these up and split them into two clean buckets, measure ten pounds in each bucket," he directed me toward the aisle with fruits and vegetables while he measured out the herbivore pellets.

"How much does an elephant eat?" I asked.

"Our girls weigh over three tons," he said. "So they'll eat more than 200 pounds of food in a single day. Most of that is hay, but then we add in pellets, fruits, and vegetables. They also drink about 50 gallons of water."

Wow. That was staggering. That amount of food is hard to picture until you're required to gather it together and put it in a truck. I was sent to get carrots, celery, bananas, beetroots, apples, and even lemons.

I was carrying buckets full of fruits and vegetables in each hand while Matt carried two buckets of pellets as we approached the back of the truck. "What do they eat in the wild?" I asked, curious.

"Anything and everything," he laughed. "Grass,

trees, fruit—whatever they can get their trunks on, as long as it's a plant."

We loaded the buckets into the back of the truck, and then Matt asked me to open the zoo's outer gate—the one the keepers and volunteers usually enter through. After he drove the truck out, I locked the gate and climbed up into the passenger side of the truck's cab—which was a literal climb, the cab is high off the ground and a step and handrail assistance are required to get in it.

We drove through the zoo parking lot to a gate on the other side of the zoo that was closer to mammal house. Though the trip was short, I had just enough time to marvel yet again at my good fortune in being there. I was nervous about the unknown—new string, new keeper . . . the fact that it was Matt—but I was also excited and felt I was right where I was meant to be.

Matt backed the truck up to the rear entrance of mammal house and we both got out. I lowered the liftgate as he unlocked the entrance to the building. But then he stopped me in the process of unloading. "Wait, come here, I want to show you something."

My heart skipped a beat as he held the door open and motioned for me to come inside. I walked by him and my breath caught.

Matt smiled at me then turned toward the hallway and yelled, "Hootie-hoot, hootie-hoot!" The elephants trumpeted in response.

Matt headed down the hallway, and I followed him with my heart in my throat. He entered the elephants' enclosure while I remained on the other side of the bars. It was apparent that Mary and Heidi were happy to see him. I marveled at his easy manner with them and the affectionate way they reached out to him with their trunks. He hugged their bent heads then walked to each chained ankle and removed their shackles, the whole time talking and cooing at them as if they were his pet dogs and not three-ton African elephants. It endeared him to me even more. Was there anything more attractive than a man who loved animals? I didn't think so.

Once they were freed, Matt gestured for me to approach the bars. "We're not supposed to do this but . . . have you ever felt an elephant's trunk?" he asked.

I shook my head and walked over tentatively. Matt held his hand out toward me and as I placed mine in his, he pulled me gently forward. Then Mary started to approach and my heart was pounding so hard — whether it was from Matt's touch or the overwhelming size of Mary, I wasn't sure. Mary's trunk started a sniffing exploration up my arm, and I couldn't suppress a giggle. She was amazing and awe-inspiring, and her size! What an overwhelming presence she had. The bars that separated us didn't feel like enough, but I didn't want Matt to know how nervous I was, and I didn't want to miss this opportunity — this incredible precious moment.

Heidi's curiosity got the better of her and she joined us. Matt maneuvered us so that Heidi's trunk could reach me. "There, now they both know who this new person is," he seemed satisfied with our introduction. "I think it's rude not to introduce you, don't you?" he asked.

I nodded.

We made our way back to the truck and started bringing everything inside. Matt took hay out into the elephants' yard and walked each elephant outside so that we could begin to clean the interior.

Like the bison yard, the inside of the elephants' enclosure was larger than it first appeared. When you see two large elephants in it, it seems small, but when it's just two humans? Enormous. As he closed the elephant-sized doors to the outside, I was reminded of the movie King Kong.

Once the work to clean inside began, and I saw the size of their piles of manure, I understood why we had brought ten trash cans with us.

"Some of their manure has hay sticking out of it," I observed. And the height and emptiness of the room carried my voice with an echo.

Matt laughed in response. "Yeah, they don't digest all of their food. It's weird," he replied.

"And yet it's still so heavy," I said, as I struggled to shovel a pile into the nearest trash can.

After we had shoveled every last bit of waste from the elephant enclosure, Matt pulled out the firehose and cleared the floor. We then took a bleach mixture and push brooms and scrubbed every inch of flooring, a process that took at least 30 minutes. Matt let me do the rinsing as he finished up the inside transfer area—this second section of their indoor enclosure was used to house the elephants when they needed to be transferred from the main section but couldn't be taken outside—such as in the case of inclement weather.

With the inside clean, Matt opened the King Kong doors to let the elephants return inside, and I ran to the anteroom to get their food buckets. Matt grabbed each of the pellet buckets and dumped them in separate spots on either side of the room, then as the girls approached their food, he chained their ankles again.

He saw the look on my face and said, "It's only

temporary. They need to stay separated from each other while they eat so we know exactly what each is getting."

He then took lemons out of each of the veggie buckets and said, "Watch this," and tossed Mary and Heidi a lemon each. We both laughed hysterically at the looks on their faces when they bit into their sour lemons.

Then I said, "Awww, I feel bad," but I couldn't stop giggling. Once I get the giggles, they just have to run their course.

"It's okay, they like them!" he said, laughing too. And as he threw them two more, I could see it was true, sour or not, they did seem to like them.

He emptied the rest of their fruit and veggie buckets onto each of their food piles, and we let them be.

* * *

After loading ten full trash cans into the back of the truck, we drove back to the main gate. This time after driving through, Matt backed the truck alongside the huge dumpster. He directed me to join him in the truck bed as the trash cans were so heavy it took two people to lift them and tip them over and into the dumpster. Afterward, we headed over to the kitchen for a break.

I was now comfortable hanging out with the keepers and other volunteers around the breakroom table, and the topic of conversation was Ringling Brothers. The circus was coming to town and the keepers were discussing whether or not they were going.

"I'm not giving them my money. They shouldn't

be forcing animals to do tricks like that. It's not natural," said Monica, and there were murmurs of agreement around the table. This was the first time I'd heard the circus spoken of with concern about how the animals were treated, and I was really interested in what the keepers thought about it.

Matt spoke up, "I need to check out their Asian elephants though, I want to see what they're doing with them."

Sherry said, "They'd never get an African elephant to do those tricks."

I was still learning the differences between the two so I tentatively asked, "Why not?" and then my face reddened as a few of the keepers chuckled.

Matt explained, "The Asian elephants are tamer. Our girls are wild!" And I could tell he approved of their wildness, perhaps seeing them as kindred spirits.

Monica rolled her eyes at him and turned to me to add, "If you see an elephant in a circus, it's most likely female, and most likely Asian. They're easier to manage." Then she turned to Matt, "But there have been African elephants in the circus, that's what Jumbo was—and male too!"

"You mean the cartoon?" Matt smirked.

"No dumbass, that was Dumbo," Monica replied.

"Well, either way, I'm going," Matt answered, and crossed his arms. "I want to see what kind of hoops they're making their elephants jump through, so to speak."

One of the other keepers, I think her name was Jody, turned to Matt. "You'll have to spy on them for us and report back," she winked.

* * *

Every afternoon, one of the elephant keepers would do a presentation at mammal house in the elephants' yard.

On this day, I stood out in the crowd in my red volunteer polo while I admired Matt talking to the crowd and putting the elephants through their routine. He had them do things like lift a leg, pull their ear flaps forward, and trumpet. Each time they completed a move, he would give them a treat.

After the show, I met him in the anteroom of mammal house. He must have still had Ringling on his mind because he explained, "The routine I do with the girls? That's not like the circus. We only make them do things that we need them to do for medical reasons. Every single move I have them do is so we can take care of them. Like raising their legs? We have to examine their feet every day and make sure there's nothing stuck in them. And then sometimes we have to trim them. Most people don't know how important that is but, with an animal this heavy, a foot problem can be life threatening."

"I had no idea, but that does make sense," I replied, feeling honored that he shared that information with me and proud that my zoo didn't make the elephants do things without a reason.

* * *

At the end of the day, as mammal house was prepped for closing and the elephants were left with their evening meal, I was the first to exit the building. A woman was standing at the observation window staring at the elephants.

She turned to me and said, "They shouldn't be

chained!"

"They're chained for their own safety at night and when they're eating," I explained.

She didn't seem satisfied with my answer. She gave me a dirty look and walked away. I rolled my eyes thinking that she just didn't understand.

Years later, the chaining would become more frequent and last longer. The excuse I was given was that the elephants were going through their teen years and had to be broken. Otherwise, they would become a danger to the keepers. I didn't know then, as I watched her storm off, that it was I who didn't understand.

The Promise of Romance

Promises are the sweetest lies.
— Unknown

I'm walking from the zoo's back gate, through the barnyard, and out to the central zoo area on my approach to mammal house. There's a mist on the ground that looks like a thick fog—almost as if I'm walking knee-deep in clouds. I become disoriented as I see an elephant approaching. Have I already reached mammal house? I'm startled now to see a rhinoceros coming at me from the right. My heart is pounding as I look for my escape route, remembering Sherry's admonishment from months ago, "Hey Jeanie, find your exit!"

Where was I going to go?

And then, just when I thought I was about to be trampled, I woke up.

The dream was so real. I'd been working in mammal house for a few months, and though I loved every minute of my time there, the work gave me an edge of anxiety that none of the other strings had created. Not even the tarantula could compare. As awe-inspiring as the animals of mammal house were, they were also incredibly dangerous. A part of me knew that as a volunteer my work was safe, but there was another part of me that was convinced otherwise. At the time, I thought that the anxious part of me was expressing itself in my dream. Later, I would wonder if it was a prophetic warning of something else.

* * *

Some days I would come in and find myself working with Holly and some days with Matt. The days with Holly were a bit of a relief because I could be myself with her. We both smoked and talked incessantly to each other throughout the day. I had gotten to know her and loved hearing stories from her home life. We were becoming good friends.

On the other hand, I was still curious about Matt and whether or not there was a possibility of something more. We'd done a lot of flirting every single time we worked together. But it never went anywhere. I made the decision that I was going to have to be the one to make the first move.

I had arrived to find Matt working the string, so I thought this might be the day. We were cleaning the indoor elephant enclosure, pushing brooms around the room, when I casually asked, "So, do you have any plans for the evening?"

Matt turned to me with a smile, "Me? No, no plans. You?"

"It's such beautiful weather, I thought I'd do something outside. I live near the bay," I replied.

"I live near the bay too," he replied.

"Really? Where?" I asked, surprised we hadn't yet talked about where we lived.

"I'm in the Williamson area. How about you?" he asked.

"I'm on the other side up Beach Road," I said, "Maybe 10 or 15 minutes away," and my heart rate increased a little.

"We could have a cookout," he said with a crooked smile.

"I'd love that," I replied. My heart was really racing now. "I'll bring the beer."

He gave me his address, and we decided to meet at his place at 6 o'clock that night. I usually left the zoo at 2 or 3, so that gave me plenty of time to get ready.

* * *

That afternoon I raced into the house, excited about my plans. My cat, Ginger, had made it a routine to smell me when I came home from the zoo, but today I didn't have time. I tossed my dirty zoo clothes into a pile on the floor and told her, "Have at it!" while I hopped into the shower.

I must have tried on six different outfits before deciding on a gray jean skirt that snapped up the front and a little white top that I borrowed from my roommate Valerie, whose clothes were much cooler than my own.

Matt had given me directions, and I left a little early so I'd have time to stop for the beer. There was a convenience store on the way where I picked up a six-pack of cold Coors Light. I still arrived early, as was my habit when going anywhere. I sat in the car for a few minutes trying to calm my nerves. This was Matt. I worked with Matt all the time. Everything was going to be fine. Oh yeah? Tell that to my sweaty palms!

I was staring up at his apartment when I saw him go out onto the balcony and tend to an outdoor grill. He hadn't seen me yet. I stepped out of the car and called up, "Hey there."

Matt smiled down at me. "Well, hello. Come on up," he motioned to the stairs. His apartment was the top half of a duplex with wooden stairs leading up to it on the outside of the building.

I climbed to the top of the stairs, and Matt met me at the front door.

"Hi," I said, grinning foolishly when he opened the door.

"Hello, again," he said and gestured for me to enter. As I walked through, I handed him the six-pack. "Care for one?" he asked.

"Yes, please," I stepped into his place and was immediately greeted by a German Shepherd.

"Jeanie, meet Stella. Stella, meet Jeanie," Matt bowed to us and turned toward the kitchen.

"Oh my goodness, look at you sweetie," I sat on the couch to get down to Stella's height without bending over in my skirt. As I sat there petting Stella, I glanced around the room. I guessed this was what you would call a bachelor pad. Hardly any furnishings, no pictures on the wall, the very bare minimum, and … not very clean. I was a bit taken aback by it all but tried not to show it.

Matt was acting differently too, and his eyes were red. As he handed me a beer the thought occurred to me that he might be stoned. "You clean up nice," he said.

I almost replied "You, too" but he looked the same. "So, how do you like living at the beach?" I asked instead. His duplex was so close to the bay that I caught a sliver of the water from the top of his steps.

"I love it. Been here four years now, and it's a great place," he replied. And seeing him here, without his zookeeper uniform on, made me realize that he did indeed have that beach bum vibe about him.

"I hope you like chicken," he said.

"Yes, I do," I replied, and I got up and followed him out to the balcony while he tended to the grill.

"You hungry?" he asked, and I thought by the look on his face that there might be a little innuendo in that question.

"Yes, I am," I stared at him knowingly, and as he began to lean toward me, I leaned towards him. Our lips met in our first kiss.

"That was nice," he said and leaned his forehead against mine.

"Yes, it was," I sighed.

"This is going to take a bit longer," he said, referring to the chicken, then led me back inside.

We sat together on the couch, and Stella sat next to Matt. He turned to her, "Jealous, girl?" and ruffled her head.

And then we kissed for a second time. And a third. And a fourth.

I tend to drink a lot when I'm nervous, and I had finished my beer. "Want another?" Matt asked.

"Yes, please," and we both got up to go to the kitchen. Dirty dishes were piled up in the sink. And I saw several baby cockroaches scattering on the counter. Why did it have to be roaches?

"Can I help prepare anything?" I asked.

He laughed and said, "Actually, all we're having is chicken, I don't have anything else."

"Oh," I was surprised and wondered if I should have offered to bring something else besides beer.

He pulled open the nearly empty fridge and grabbed two more bottles of beer, handing me one while he went back for barbeque sauce.

We made our way back to the balcony and he dumped some sauce onto the chicken then put his arms around me as I leaned against the balcony railing. We kissed some more.

Matt pulled the chicken from the grill and since his small dinette table was stacked full of miscellaneous junk, we sat on the couch to eat it. I kept my plate held high because Stella was now more interested in our food than she was in her dad.

The chicken was red and bleeding near the bone, but I didn't say anything.

After dinner and another beer, our heavy petting session went into overdrive, and we had sex right there on the living room floor, in front of Stella.

* * *

By the time I left it was nearing midnight, but my sister Zoey was still up when I got home.

"So how was it?" she asked with a knowing smile.

"Interesting . . ." I forced myself to sound cheerful about it and proceeded to tell her about my evening. But the more I recalled, the more I realized how different the night had gone from what I had expected. And how different Matt was from who I had imagined. As I talked to her, the more I became aware of my disappointment.

Zoey said, "So let me get this straight, you think he was stoned, you ate raw chicken, and his apartment has roaches?"

"Well, when you put it that way ... that pretty much sums it up, yes" I laughed, but I felt like crying.

"And . . . why did you have sex with him?" she asked with raised eyebrows.

"I don't know . . . he's different at the zoo, okay?" I said defensively, but I also had my doubts.

A Growing Friendship

We are kindred spirits, forged in different
fires but kindred.
— Aaron Polson

A week went by and I hadn't heard from Matt. Emotionally, I was on a roller coaster. I wanted to hear from him; I didn't want to hear from him. I didn't know what I felt from one day to the next. Part of me felt guilty that I had second thoughts—after all, I had had a crush on the guy forever, we flirted all the time, and I did have sex with him. But another part of me said that I had been overlooking everything about him that bothered me, trying to make him into something and someone that he wasn't. The reality, perhaps, was that I had fallen for a fantasy.

I was too embarrassed to go to the zoo that next weekend. And then I was angry with myself for not having gone.

The following weekend, I arrived at the zoo full of anxiety about running into him but determined to continue with my commitment to volunteer. I loved the zoo, and I loved my work there. So what if Matt hadn't called? I hadn't wanted him to, had I? We had had our fling. I needed to face seeing him again.

As it turned out, all my worry was for nothing. To my great relief, Matt wasn't working. I worked string 3 with Holly, who was now far enough along in her pregnancy that she was showing. This was her second child.

"Holly, let me get that," I gently brushed her aside as she attempted to move a trash can full of manure.

"I'm fine," she insisted. "I worked through my first pregnancy, and I'll work through this one."

Admittedly, she was in great shape with muscular arms and legs and just the hint of a beach ball rising from her abdomen. If you saw her from behind, you'd never guess she was pregnant. But I felt sure her doctor wouldn't want her moving these trash cans. Manure was heavy.

"Well, let's not take any chances," I said, and grabbed the trash can away from her anyway. "Take advantage of me while I'm here," I called back to her as I maneuvered the can to the end of the aisle.

I was so glad I had returned, and I vowed to myself to keep coming so I could continue to help her no matter what was going on with me and Matt. My purpose at the zoo and my desire to be here had nothing to do with him in the beginning, and it should have nothing to do with him now.

After I rolled all of the trash cans onto the truck bed, we drove to the dumpster where I had to accept Holly's help, because it was a two-person job to lift and empty each barrel over the side of the truck. But I was happy to be there to help her.

During my break, while smoking on the rock where Matt had first approached me, I noticed a spider monkey in a small enclosure. I stomped out my cigarette and as I approached the cage, the monkey pressed his belly against the fence and began grunting. Monkers.

"Monkers!" I exclaimed as I reached over to rub his belly.

"You darling handsome thing. What are you

doing back here all alone?" I was confused and concerned about him.

After our break, we replenished the truck with supplies for the tapirs, rhinos, and the sole hippo. On our drive back over to mammal house, I asked Holly about Monkers.

"Do you know what he's doing in the back like that?" I asked.

"Jeanie, he's old. Reggie took over his troop, and Monkers was too old for any other zoo to want him. So they moved him to docents," Holly explained.

"But he's not a docent animal, right? I mean they aren't taking him out to show him to schools or anything?" I asked.

"No, he's basically just living out his old age," she replied.

"But alone?" I asked. I was heartbroken.

"He must be twenty-six or twenty-seven years old now, he isn't expected to live much longer," she continued. But I could tell she was bothered by it too.

* * *

We arrived at mammal house and walked down to the rhinos with a plan to clean them first. Both rhinos were out in their yard so Holly pressed the button that would close their outer doors. The doors stopped halfway, unable to close completely because of hay and mud that was blocking the track.

Holly said, "I need you to stay next to the button, and as soon as I give you the signal, shut the doors."

I was nervous as I watched her walk across the room to the outer doors. The rhinos were just on the other side, and I marveled at her bravery.

"Holly, one of the rhinos is walking this way," I warned. She had her head bent to her task and was using her foot to push the grime out of the door track.

"Holly, I mean it," I yelled anxiously. "You need to hurry and get out of there."

She called back, "Push the button!" and I did so quickly, relieved as the double doors came together.

"Oh my God, I can't believe how brave you are," I said.

"I don't even think they'd hurt me," she said, "at least not on purpose. The problem is their near-sightedness. They could charge me just because they see my movement but don't realize that it's me."

"Well on purpose or not, those horns look dangerous," I said.

"You know, some zoos overseas have to cut their rhino's horns for fear of poaching," she told me.

"Poaching? At a zoo? That's awful," I said, thinking how killing a captive animal must be one of the most cowardly acts there is.

"Yes, it happens. Some people are convinced that their horns are aphrodisiacs," she explained.

"That's ridiculous!" I said. "What do they do with it?"

"They grind it into a powder and consume it like tea or something," she answered.

"Humans!" I said with exasperation, and she nodded in agreement.

We scooped poop and cleaned the rhino enclosure area together, just as we had done with the elephants. And, despite her protests, I again took on the job of rolling the trash cans outside and getting them into the back of the truck.

We smoked and chatted companionably

afterward. "I feel guilty for smoking, but the doctor said if I can't quit to at least limit it, and I've dropped down to five a day."

"My mom smoked more than a pack a day through seven pregnancies," I told her, hoping to alleviate some of her guilt. "I turned out okay, right?" I asked jokingly.

She stubbed her cigarette out halfway through. "I'll save the rest for later. I need you to do me a favor."

"Of course," I said. "Name it."

"Normally, I'd have to get another keeper to help me, but since you're here, I need you to do the serval cats alone … because of my pregnancy," she explained.

"Oh, I can do that!" I said, relieved that it was something I already knew how to do though I had never done it all by myself.

"Great, let's go," and we walked over to the truck bed where she pulled a bucket forward. "Here's their food." She handed me a plastic bag with bloody meat inside.

"What kind of meat is that?" I asked as it was like nothing I'd ever seen before.

"Venison," she answered. "Come on, I'll walk you over," and we crossed a broad path to reach the serval cat exhibit on the other side.

Holly unlocked the door, and we walked inside together. She said, "I'll transfer them outside so you can clean their indoor habitat."

"No problem," I said.

"Once you clean, just leave their food in the bins and transfer them back in. Then you clean the outside. I'll go take care of the tapirs," and she left me alone.

When my indoor work was complete, I opened their guillotine doors and let them back in. I eyed them obsessively even though there were only two — making sure they were both inside because an accidental miss with these cats would be dangerous. As I closed their doors, I thought about Rufus, the one-armed gibbon.

I loved visiting the cats. They looked like tiny leopards with giant ears. But their only interest was in the slabs of meat I had left them so I walked around the corner to access their outer yard. I recalled the first time I had worked in the serval cat area and how Matt had asked me if I was pregnant.

He had laughed at the shocked look on my face and took pleasure in explaining why he had to ask. "Don't get me wrong, you don't look pregnant," he winked. "But pregnant women aren't supposed to handle cat feces. They can get a parasitic infection called toxoplasmosis."

"Oh," I laughed. "I had no idea. Is that just wild cats?" I wondered because I had had cats all my life and had never heard about this.

"Nope, all cats," he said.

"Well, I have a cat at home so good thing I'm not pregnant," I kind of laughed.

The memory reminded me of the last time I had seen him, and my heart fluttered and sank.

I met Holly back in mammal house as she was finishing up with the tapirs, and we worked the rest of string 3 together.

Behind Closed Doors

Animals are reliable, many full of love,
true in their affections, predictable in
their actions, grateful and loyal. Difficult
standards for people to live up to.
— Alfred Montapert

One sunny day, Holly and I were cleaning the rhino yard together. Like the elephants, the rhinos created a good amount of heavy excrement, but the thing I found interesting in their case was that they always did their business in the same spot in their yard. How smart is that? We were shoveling the pile into buckets when Holly told me we had a new volunteer coming that morning and asked me to keep my eye on her. I was happy to do so but curious about her concerns.

"I think she might be a spy from PETA," she explained.

"A spy? But why?" I asked.

"I have my suspicions. Something just isn't right about her . . ." she continued.

"But why would PETA send a spy to this zoo?" I asked. I thought we were doing pretty good. The zoo had gotten the AZA accreditation it had sought so it was meeting higher standards now, unlike its days of keeping captive chimpanzees.

"PETA hates zoos, don't you know that?" she asked.

"I know they're against circuses and concerned

about conditions for animals in captivity, I just wondered why you thought they would come to this particular zoo?" I had actually joined PETA and got their magazine but figured now wasn't a good time to mention it.

Holly just shrugged.

The new volunteer, Sara, joined us in mammal house and seemed completely innocent of whatever spying Holly thought she might be doing, but ironically, the day she came was the same day that a big load of clay had been dumped into the elephants' yard, and it was all Holly could do to keep them from eating it. It was making her a nervous wreck.

"Why are they eating dirt?" I whispered to her.

"I don't know, it might just be because it's something new in their yard . . ." I could tell she wasn't sure.

"Will it hurt them?" I asked.

She hesitated."I don't think so, as long as they don't eat too much of it." Then she added almost to herself, "I'm going to have to get in there and start spreading it quickly before they make themselves sick."

I would later learn that elephants and other animals may eat clay if they are missing sodium in their diet. They are attracted to its saltiness.

While Holly hurried to spread out the clay, I worked alongside Sara.

Many of the exhibits at the zoo had signs posted that read, "Species Survival Plan - The animals in this exhibit are threatened with extinction and part of the Species Survival Plan." Mammal house had these plaques for the elephants and the rhinos, and Sara asked me about it.

"What exactly is the Species Survival Plan," she

wondered.

I answered her in the same way I had heard the zookeepers address it, "The Species Survival Plan breeds endangered animals in captivity to help them survive and not go extinct. Accredited members of the Association of Zoos and Aquariums can take part in the program and this zoo is now accredited and doing their part." I thought, if Sara is a PETA spy then I think she'll be happy with this answer. At that time, I was proud that my zoo was a part of that program.

* * *

It was fall again, my favorite time of year at the zoo. I had worked with Matt twice in the last couple of months. We were cordial to each other, both of us acting as if nothing had happened between us. But on this particular crisp morning, I had arrived to find Holly.

We had just finished loading the truck when Holly turned to me, "I'm so glad you came in. My belly's getting in the way more and more these days," she patted her growing baby bump.

I told her, "I'd like to get your schedule so that I can make sure I'm coming in when you're on the string and not Matt."

She turned and looked at me kind of funny so I tried to explain, "I mean, he's fine, it's just I don't think he needs me as much as you do..." When her look didn't change, I continued, "Just while you're pregnant . . . I know you're a badass . . ."

She shook her head, "No, it's not that … it's just …" She hesitated and then lowered her voice. "I know I shouldn't be telling you this, but …"

"But, what?" I exclaimed. I could tell she was weighing her words. "What is it?" I insisted.

"He was caught with a volunteer," she whispered.

My heart missed a beat, and then it felt as if it jumped into my throat while my stomach did a flip-flop. "Uh . . . uh," I stammered. My mind was racing trying to make sense of what she'd just said. I searched her face for hidden meaning. Was she talking about me? Did they know about me and Matt? Was dating a volunteer against the rules?

She continued conspiratorially, "In the hay barn."

"What?!" I almost yelled, and Holly shushed me.

"Come on, I'll tell you about it on the way," she grabbed my sleeve and pulled me toward the truck.

As we both walked to either side of the truck's cab, my mind was an explosion of thoughts. Caught. In the barn. With a volunteer. What on earth?

As soon as we closed the truck doors, Holly started talking and driving at the same time.

"You know the keeper, John?" She asked.

I quickly nodded.

"Well apparently, John went to the hay barn to, you know, get hay?" she said. "That's what it's there for . . ."

"Yes, yes," I gestured, urging her to continue.

"There was Matt . . . with a volunteer named Crystal . . ." She stopped, "Do you know her?" she asked.

"Crystal, Crystal . . . no, I can't say that I do," I answered.

"Well it turns out, Crystal is like 16 years old," Holly sounded disgusted.

"Oh my God, you have got to be kidding me," I felt shocked and embarrassed and angry all at the same time.

"No, I'm not. So . . . they were doing something

they shouldn't have been doing and . . . now Matt's been fired," she said with emphasis.

"Well, I should hope so!" I stated.

We sat in silence for about ten seconds before the conversation continued.

"What about her parents, how did they react?" I asked tentatively.

"I don't know," Holly replied. "I've told you everything I know. I don't think they were having sex, I think they were, you know, making out."

"Ugh. What a dumbass," I said, exasperated. And the more I thought about it, the angrier I got. "You know those elephants really love him," I said, and I wasn't sure what upset me the most, but I hated that he would do something that jeopardized the emotional lives of those elephants! They always got so excited to see him. And now, who could explain to them where their favorite person went? No one.

"Yeah, I know. He always was good with animals, especially the girls, but rumor has it that he's gone to Hawthorn," she said.

"Hawthorn?" I asked. "What's Hawthorn?"

"It's a place up in Illinois that trains elephants for circuses," she informed me.

"Circuses!" I yelled. "But Matt hates circuses!"

"I guess he doesn't hate them anymore," she paused. "Or maybe he thinks he'll help the elephants there," she shrugged. "Beats me."

"That is so strange. Wow. I don't know what to think anymore," I sighed.

"People can't be trusted. Give me an animal over a human any day," she said.

"Amen to that, sister," I said, still in a daze.

Zylah the Hippo

There is an eagle in me that wants to soar,
and there is a hippopotamus in me that
wants to wallow in the mud.
— Carl Sandburg

I had just returned from my solo duties at the serval cat house, something I'd been doing since that first day Holly had requested it of me, and I was heading down to clean Zylah's area. This was the most stressful part of my day. Holly had already educated me about the dangers of hippos. A species I used to find so cute and endearing, I now respectfully feared with all my being. Holly could reach her hand right into Zylah's wide gaping mouth and pat her tongue, but that didn't make me feel any safer.

The problem was the setup of Zylah's housing. Hippos need water, lots of it. They will spend sixteen hours a day submerged up to the nostrils and eyeballs. Zylah's pool, which was just wide and long enough to cover her entire body, took up almost her entire indoor enclosure area and was very deep—probably a foot or more over my head. Each day, the pool would be drained for cleaning, while Zylah waited . . . impatiently . . . outside.

If you were down in the pool, the only way to get out was via the steps. Those steps faced the back and Zylah's outside door. The door that wouldn't close all the way. Too many years of grime and rust had left about a four-inch gap. Zylah would peer into that gap from the outside. And as if her insistent stare wasn't enough, she would follow it with a bang, bang, bang from the side of her snout to the metal doors. Unless Zylah was preoccupied with something else in her yard, I could count on heart palpitations during the entire time that I cleaned her pool. Of course, not wanting to appear inept, or cowardly, I had never told Holly about my fear.

I had not forgotten Sherry's advice to always look for my escape. The problem with Zylah's pool was, there was no escape. If the day ever came that she got through those doors while I was scrubbing the bottom of her pool, I was sunk. No pun intended.

I was down in the bottom of the pool when I heard Holly walk in. I looked up at her.

"Did I ever tell you Zylah's story?" she asked.

I shook my head.

"All that talk about Matt going to Hawthorn reminded me. . . Zylah came from a circus," she said.

"Wow, I didn't know they had hippos in circuses," I was listening but kept scrubbing. Holly's presence made me feel safer, so I wanted to try to get the pool done before she left me alone again.

Holly sat on the slanted sill of the big display window, "This was years ago in Las Vegas — she came to the zoo in 1975," she waved her hand backward over her shoulder, "so this was way back."

I paused, broom in hand. "What did she do?" I asked, curious. "In the circus, I mean."

"She used to pull a wagon, and in the wagon was a goat," she smiled, relishing the picture she painted.

"Okay ..." I said, wondering now if she was pulling my leg.

"Zylah and the goat were the best of friends. They

didn't just perform the circus act together, the circus kept them together all the time. They slept together; they ate together. Best buddies and companions," she explained.

"That's interesting," I kept sweeping.

"One night, the circus's tiger escaped from his cage and … he attacked and ate the goat." She paused.

"Oh, no!" I stopped. She had my full attention now.

"You know how I told you how fierce hippos are?" she reminded me, "Well Zylah went on a rampage! She destroyed the circus in her efforts to kill the tiger."

"Wow, is that really true?" I responded, still not sure if I could believe such a fantastical tale.

"Yes, it is!" she exclaimed. "That's how she came to be at the zoo."

I shook my head. "That is one crazy story," I said.

"I know! But it's true. And I hate seeing her all alone here. I have tried to get zoo management to put a goat in here with her. I really don't think she would hurt him. . . but they won't do it," she frowned.

I laughed. "Holly, really? Put a goat with Zylah? I can see why they said no," I resumed scrubbing. I was working down there in fear for my life, and I couldn't imagine the stress that would put on a little goat.

"She's a vegetarian!" she added by way of explanation as she walked out.

"Do you think the goat will know that?" I yelled back to her.

Family Time

The bond that links your true family is
not one of blood, but of respect and joy in
each other's life.
— Richard Bach

Holly and I had become good friends and she
invited me to join her and her family for an
afternoon backyard barbeque. I was excited to spend
time with her outside of the zoo and was pondering
what to wear when I ended up in the same outfit I
had worn to Matt's. A tank top and a gray skirt.

I knew Holly lived near the ocean but was
surprised to see her home was on stilts, like the
many beach vacation rental homes in the area. I
hadn't realized that some people lived in them all
year long, and I thought she was very lucky.

I arrived carrying a six pack, and she welcomed
me as I made my way up the outside stairs. "Wow,
you clean up nice," she said as she held the door
open for me.

"So do you," I laughed. This was beginning to
feel reminiscent of my trip to Matt's house. And
like Matt, Holly had seen me at my worst — sweaty,
dirty, and ankle-deep in elephant manure. One can
only go up from there.

As I walked in, I saw there was a great view of the
ocean from her living room window. "Wow, your
place is amazing," I exclaimed.

"Thanks, we really love it," she replied modestly.

"I should say so!" I said as her oldest child came running into the room. "What a great place to raise kids," I added.

Her husband followed after her son and she included him by saying, "We spend a lot of time making sandcastles on the beach." Then added, "Jeanie this is T.J.; T.J. this is Jeanie."

I reached my hand out and said, "It's so nice to meet you. I've heard a lot about you."

T.J. shook my hand, "Same here."

I knew from Holly that he was in the Navy. She had once joked that between her profession as an elephant keeper and his profession as a Navy Seal, their insurance premiums were through the roof. What I didn't know was that she had invited one of his Navy comrades to join us.

T.J. turned to Holly, "Mark should be here in less than ten. I'll go get the grill started," and he was out the door.

"Holly…" I said slowly. "Who is Mark?"

"Oh, he's just a friend of T.J.'s from work," she shrugged nonchalantly.

"Just a friend from work, huh? He wouldn't happen to be a single friend from work, would he?" I raised one eyebrow.

"Actually . . . he's going through a divorce," she explained.

"Oh, I see," I exaggerated an eye roll.

"It's okay, you don't have to like him," she was emphatic. "I just thought it would be nice for him to have some company . . . and you, too!"

"I appreciate it, really," I said. I didn't want her to feel bad or guilty, but the whole Matt thing was still pretty fresh. Of course, she had no way of knowing that as I had been too embarrassed to tell her about it.

When Mark arrived, I learned he had two children, and I knew immediately that I was not interested. I loved children but did not want to get involved with a father of young kids going through a divorce. My mom had remarried after my father's death and so I witnessed firsthand what a stressful situation that could be and was too young to consider having that in my life.

We all spent a companionable evening together, and I enjoyed strengthening my friendship with Holly, but the match-making was a fail. During the evening, Holly and I made plans for me to invite my family to come to the zoo for a behind-the-scenes tour.

* * *

Instead of volunteering on this beautiful Sunday morning, I was arriving at the zoo with my mom, my Aunt Alice, my sister Melissa, and my nephew Harold. I was over the moon excited to be able to share some of my experiences behind the scenes at mammal house, where I had made a plan for us to meet Holly after lunch.

First, we made our way around the rest of the zoo where I was able to offer insights and stories about Billy Bob (yes, Mom, that is the monkey who bit me on the boob, he was much smaller then); the tragic loss of half of Rufus' arm; Diana the Bison and the loss of her herd; the duck pond (see the nesting boxes on the island?); what the raptors eat (you don't want to know); and so much more. We settled down to an early lunch near the barnyard animals where I explained that sometimes the female goat humps the other goats. It's not about sex but dominance.

Soon we were headed to my favorite place, and I found myself knocking on the outer door of mammal house.

Holly welcomed us as we came streaming through the doorway into the suddenly too small anteroom. She had brought some extra treats with her today. "I call them my secret weapons," she said mischievously and motioned for us to follow her.

We made our way all the way to the end of mammal house to Zylah's enclosure first. Holly relished telling the story of Zylah's destruction of her circus and the fierceness of hippos, and then she smiled broadly, "Watch this."

She held a loaf of bread up high for Zylah to see. Zylah made her way to Holly — who was protected by three huge metal poles between them — and opened her mouth as wide as it would go. Holly laid the entire loaf of bread on her huge tongue, then quickly backed away. Zylah closed her mouth and swallowed the loaf whole while my family oohed and aahed and exclaimed over Holly's bravery.

Next, we made our way to the rhinos. When they were indoors like this, I could reach in and rub their ears, and I did so then to show my family how their ears rotate independently of each other. Holly explained, "Their excellent hearing helps to compensate for their poor eyesight."

Holly gave me a handful of grains and instructed me to hold my hand out flat for them to eat off of it, which I did for the first time. I was full of fear but also had my family as an audience, so I couldn't turn her down, though I think I almost gave my mom a heart attack. I felt the rhinos' broad flat lips suck the grains off of my hands and let out a nervous giggle.

For the elephants, we were not allowed to have

contact — though I did tell my family about the experience I had the first day I met them when they had explored my presence with their trunks. Holly went to them and handed each a lemon and we laughed at their sour faces. She also shared information about their diets and how every day each elephant consumes five bales of hay, fifteen pounds of grain, loads of fruits and vegetables, and as much as fifty gallons of water!

After our private tour, Holly was due to do the elephant show in the yard. As we watched, I repeated what Matt had taught me, that—unlike circuses—they only make the elephants do things — like lifting their feet and trunks and opening their ear flaps — so that they can do medical and wellness checks.

Tiger Twins

It is not part of a true culture to tame
tigers, any more than it is to make sheep
ferocious.
— Henry David Thoreau

I'd been volunteering at the zoo for several
years when I arrived one day to find that Holly
was one of the zookeepers in charge of the care and
feeding of two Siberian tiger cubs. She told me about
them during our morning routine at mammal house.

"Where did they come from?" I recalled how zoos
sometimes sell their baby animals and wondered if
that's how our zoo had gotten them.

"The black market," Holly almost whispered.
"Apparently, a private owner had them, and they
were trying to sell them. They were confiscated by
the U.S. Fish and Wildlife Services, who asked us if
we could take care of them."

"What happened to their mom?" I wondered aloud.

"We don't know. They didn't have her, just the
cubs," she sounded just as worried about what may
have happened to her as I was.

"How old are they?" I was trying to imagine what
they might look like.

"They're young, about four weeks old. Monica's
been taking them home with her for a week or so,"
she explained. I recalled how Lisa had told me that
zookeepers would sometimes take baby animals
home with them to give them around-the-clock care.

"We'll go see them mid-morning. We need to feed them," she said excitedly.

* * *

The tiger cubs were being kept in the same administrative building where I had gone to attend my volunteer orientation. I hadn't had a reason to visit it since then but I had a better idea of what must go on in there now. I was working at a nonprofit and I imagined the zoo had a lot of similar administrative tasks . . . marketing, human resources, accounting, and membership. In addition, they had a veterinary clinic.

We went in through the back door and walked down a hallway and passed several offices before arriving at our destination. Holly was petite but strong, and despite our height difference, I nearly had to run to keep up with her. I thoughts, someone's excited to see the cubs again!

When we walked into their room, I could see why. They were absolutely adorable, and we were oohing and aahing all over them in no time. I was so surprised by their size. I had pictured kittens, but a four-week-old tiger cub is much larger than even a full-grown house cat.

Holly asked me to play with them while she prepared their bottles. Not a problem. I was on it. "My pleasure," I said.

I dropped to the floor to greet them and was immediately pounced on by both cubs. I started to laugh as I tried to give them both attention. They were not yet old enough for their stripes to take on that bold defined look; they were all fuzziness and paws. Very big paws. While their size was nothing like a typical kitten, their behavior was about the same, only with much larger teeth and longer claws.

Holly joined us on the floor, handing me one of the bottles as she sat down.

I beamed at her.

"Yes, you get to feed one," she smiled back. "Hold her like this," she reached over and grabbed one of the cubs and steadied her into a standing position then angled the bottle toward her mouth. The cub latched onto the bottle ferociously. I grabbed the other cub and followed suit.

What a precious moment.

"Do they have names?" I asked as I struggled to keep both bottle and baby steady and laughed at my cub's enthusiasm.

"Yes, let me see …" Holly stared at my cub, and then at hers. "You have Cleopatra."

"How can you tell?" I was surprised by her quick identification.

"See the collar colors?" she pointed to my cub, then hers. "And I have Anubis."

After the cubs were fed they abruptly fell asleep, and we made our exit, returning to mammal house to finish our morning chores.

* * *

Feeding and playing with the cubs was a ritual I would come to enjoy until one week when I showed up and Holly told me that the cubs were no longer allowed human contact. Cleopatra and Anubis were older now and they needed to regain a bit of their wildness. I understood this on an intellectual level but emotionally I was saddened by it.

The serval cats were sold to another zoo, and

the cubs took their place in that exhibit, having exceeded the serval cats' appeal and ability to bring in a crowd. A campaign was started with local Exxon gas stations to raise money for a larger habitat for the tigers, and the twins quickly became the most popular attraction at the zoo.

Part Three: An Awakening

The earth does not belong to man, man
belongs to the earth. All things are
connected like the blood that unites us all.
Man did not weave the web of life, he is
merely a strand in it. Whatever he does to
the web, he does to himself.
— Chief Seattle

The Baby Elephant in the Room

Some people talk to animals. Not many
listen though. That's the problem.
— A.A. Milne

The power of the tigers to draw a crowd inspired the zoo's plans for growth that I first learned about from Holly.

One day as we were working in mammal house Holly confided in me, "I'm hoping they'll let me impregnate one of the girls."

I stopped working and turned to her in confusion, "What on earth are you talking about?"

"The elephants, of course!" She looked at me like I was the one who was crazy.

"I know Mary will let me do it, I will just artificially inseminate her, and then she'll get to have a baby." She paused then added, "In nature, all the females take care of the babies, including the aunts. I think Heidi will make a great aunt, and. . ."

I interrupted her stream of words, "Wait a minute . . . slow down. Explain to me how this works. How would you artificially inseminate Mary?"

"Zoos do it, Jeanie, it's how they sometimes make babies. We just need the semen of an African bull elephant . . ."

I stopped her again, "I'm afraid to ask, but how do you get the semen from an African bull elephant?"

Holly hesitated, "They do it with, umm, massage." She had the good grace to look embarrassed but then she quickly became earnest. "It's a lot better than putting the male through the stress of transport and it's not like we have room for a male here. They're very difficult to manage."

"Unless they're having a . . . massage," I joked sarcastically.

"Seriously, though, wouldn't it be great to have a baby elephant here?" she was animated again. "The girls would be so happy, and you and I could help take care of it!"

"Of course, it would be awesome for us . . . but Holly, think about the baby. Is this really a place for a baby elephant to grow up? Look how small the yard is, and there's no room in here..." I turned all the way around with my arms wide.

"The city has already approved an expansion. The zoo will have a whole new area dedicated to Africa, and Asia too — both the elephants and the tigers are going to get bigger yards and housing," she told me.

I hesitated, "That sounds great . . . they can all use more space."

"I know it's small now but after the expansion, with a whole new area dedicated to Africa, it will be perfect. I'm going to suggest it to management. And Mary trusts me, I know she'll let me do the insemination."

I simply replied, "Well, good luck." But my heart wasn't in it.

* * *

I had reached a tipping point. It was as if the baby elephant conversation was the proverbial last straw. I'd go weeks without volunteering; those weeks soon became months.

I had long defended the zoo's Species Survival Plan. The problem was, as I came to see it, most animals confined in zoos are not endangered. And the ones who are endangered are not being bred for release into their natural habitats. Elephants in the program, like our zoo's own elephants, would be impossible to release in the wild. They had spent the majority of their lives in captivity and there was really no wild place for them to go.

Holly's campaign to get permission to artificially inseminate one of the African elephants failed, but it had an unintended effect. It opened my eyes to the futility of having these animals listed under the Species Survival Plan. In fact, it opened my eyes to the needlessness of having these animals in zoos at all. What is the point of this species' survival if they are to be denied everything that is natural to them and never experience the wild? What I had eventually come to see was that the Species Survival Plan was really more of a "Zoo Survival Plan."

I was now looking at every exhibit through the eyes of a baby elephant. And all of them came up short. If the zoo's enclosures were not, in my point of view, good enough for a baby elephant, why were they good enough for the two adults who were currently occupying it? These two elephants had actually been stolen from the wild when they themselves were babies. That tragedy was finally apparent to me.

Yes, the zoo had gotten its accreditation, and there were some really dedicated keepers who loved and cared for the animals — Holly was chief among them. But no one seemed to be looking at it from the animals' point of view.

I couldn't clean Zylah's pool now without realizing how small it was and how she'd been alone for decades. Though I saw him less frequently, the same could be said for No Name, the sea lion, who should be basking in the sun on a Pacific coastline with hundreds, or even thousands, of his own kind instead of living his life in solitary confinement. I couldn't look at the rhinos without wondering what they would do if they could actually run free–I'd see them start to run but their area was so small they always stopped short. And the tigers? Those cubs were full-grown now and their exhibit could not even begin to mimic the natural habitat of the largest feline in the world. I was glad that they had been taken from the black market and given a life that didn't include cub petting and declawing and God knows what other horribleness might have awaited them had they not been confiscated by the U.S. Fish and Wildlife Services, but they deserved more. They deserved to never have been on the black market in the first place. I thought of Monkers, separated from his family and kept in a small cage in the back of the zoo — now in his late 20s, the same age as me. I thought of Diana, who had lost her entire herd to an "accidental" overdose. I thought of all the animals bred at the zoo only to be taken from their families and sold to other zoos, or worse, fed to other zoo animals. I thought of it all, and I couldn't see the zoo — or any zoo — the same way again.

Epilogue

The human spirit needs places where
nature has not been rearranged by the
hand of man.
— Anonymous

Shortly after I stopped volunteering at the zoo, Zylah the hippo died. A necropsy revealed an obstruction in her digestive system caused by a racquetball, probably thrown into her yard by a zoo visitor. She never did get a companion, goat or otherwise, having lived alone at the zoo for over 20 years. That's 20 years of solitary confinement for an animal who is social by nature. Had she lived in the wild, she would have had a huge family and spent so much time in water that she'd be called amphibious. Like a giant frog with a mouth about as proportionately wide.

It would take over a decade and millions of dollars from both the city and the zoo's own fundraising efforts before the expansion would take place. The new African area would include a "Savannah" enclosure to allow animals room to roam. Once the African expansion was complete, I thought I would check up on my old friends and see if the larger exhibits helped me to feel better about the zoo. They didn't.

One of the first places I visited housed two baby giraffes. They were located inside a barn to protect them from the weather so they were unable to take advantage of their fake Savannah at the time that I saw them. Zoo visitors could get up close to them because of an elevated walkway. They looked utterly fragile. A couple of months later, I learned that both giraffe babies had died. My heart broke. In the wild, a male giraffe would remain with his mom until he is over a year old and a female would stay near her mom for the rest of her life. These giraffes were taken from their mom and sold to this zoo, and for what? A few extra ticket sales and untimely death? As the years went by, the zoo would acquire and breed adult giraffes. Their babies would not always survive.

The zoo's elephants were joined by a new female. Heidi and Mary had been at the zoo since 1976, both arriving at the tender age of three. At the age of 38, Heidi became ill and had to be euthanized. A few years later, in order to meet the new guidelines of AZA accreditation that said zoos must maintain elephant herds of three or more members, the decision was made to move Mary and her new companion, Jill, to a warmer climate where they could reside with other elephants. Shortly after their arrival at their new zoo in Florida, Jill was killed in a confrontation with another elephant. Mary would die a short time later from a twisting of her bowel.

The Siberian tiger sisters got a somewhat larger enclosure funded by a campaign partnership with local Exxon gas stations, but they did not live long enough to see the Asian expansion that would have greatly increased their grounds. They both died of cancer within months of each other. They were 18 years old.

I would learn through news articles and publications published by People for the Ethical

Treatment of Animals (PETA)[1] that Hawthorn Corporation, where Matt was rumored to have gone, was notorious for its failure to meet animal welfare standards for the elephants and tigers it housed and rented to circuses. The Illinois-based company, owned by John Cuneo, was fined by the United States Department of Agriculture (USDA) and had its license suspended twice. Cuneo admitted to numerous willful violations of the federal Animal Welfare Act, and the USDA ordered Hawthorn to relinquish sixteen endangered Asian elephants — in addition to one who was determined to be in "imminent danger of death." PETA had provided the USDA with information that showed neglect of the animals and unsupervised handling by the public: People fed and touched elephants from Hawthorn who had tuberculosis (TB).

Afterword

The only creature on earth whose natural
habitat is a zoo is the zookeeper.
— Robert Brault

The zoo had to make several changes in order to become accredited by the Association of Zoos and Aquariums (AZA). Those changes involved modifying habitats to better suit each species and allowing animals adequate and species-appropriate space. In some cases, the zoo had to sell animals because they could not properly accommodate them.

The current process of accreditation by the AZA, according to its own website is that each institution that requests accreditation is: evaluated by recognized experts in the profession and is measured against the established standards and best practices of that profession . . . AZA has been the primary accrediting body for zoos and aquariums for over 40 years. U.S. agencies such as OSHA and the USDA consider AZA standards as the "national" standard, and they refer to AZA standards when evaluating institutions. AZA's rigorous, scientifically based and publicly-available standards examine the zoo or aquarium's entire operation, including animal welfare, veterinary care, conservation, education, guest services, physical facilities, safety, staffing, finance, and governing body.[2]

So an AZA-accredited zoo at least has standards.

However, that doesn't prevent breeding, for which the AZA also offers guidelines. Again, according to the AZA's own website, "The mission of an Association of Zoos and Aquariums (AZA) cooperatively managed Species Survival Plan® (SSP) Program is to manage an ex situ species population with the interest and cooperation of AZA-accredited zoos and aquariums, Certified Related Facilities (CRFs), and Sustainability Partners . . . [that] develops a Breeding and Transfer Plan that identifies population goals and recommendations to manage a genetically diverse, demographically varied, and biologically sound population."[3] In other words, the AZA's SSP breeding program breeds animals to be kept in captivity by AZA-accredited facilities. And the one thing that it cares about is ensuring that there is genetic diversity so as not to inbreed closely related animals.

Zoos breed animals in order to keep drawing in crowds. Baby animals are always popular with the public that zoos serve. But when baby after baby is born, what happens to the growing adult population? By its name, you would think the Species Survival Plan meant that animals were bred and released into the wild in order to help their species thrive in their natural environment. That's what I used to think.

In 2014, the Copenhagen Zoo in Denmark came under fire when it openly killed a healthy 18-month old giraffe, dissected and butchered him in front of a crowd, and then fed him to the zoo's lions. Why did the zoo choose to kill this giraffe in spite of numerous offers to rescue him and thousands of signatures on an online petition? Inbreeding worries. "Copenhagen Zoo's giraffes are part of an international breeding programme which aims at ensuring a healthy giraffe population in European zoos."[4]

One month later, that same zoo euthanized four African lions "to make way for a new male lion from the Givskud Zoo, also in Denmark."[5] Again, the excuse given was risk of inbreeding.

According to numerous reports in November 2021, the European Association of Zoos and Aquaria (EAZA) began considering a cull of adult male western lowland gorillas, even though they are critically endangered in the wild.[6] EAZA is the body that regulates most of the zoos in Europe–like the AZA in America. The problem? Overbreeding in zoos, too many males, and no place to release them in the wild.

While zoos without governing bodies are far worse for animals than those that are accredited, as long as breeding continues, there will always be too many adult animals with no place to go.

A proper sanctuary, such as those accredited by the Global Federation of Animal Sanctuaries,[7] does not allow any breeding and therefore offers its animals the lifelong care that zoos are not able to afford to them.

The least we can do is not to frequent zoos. Just don't buy that ticket. There are innumerable ways to learn about animals these days without helping to support the system that imprisons them in order to feed itself.

Some accredited sanctuaries offer in-person visits that do not interfere with the lives of the animals in their care. Others offer webcam views of their inhabitants. Streaming services and online resources like Netflix and National Geographic are full of educational documentaries that show the real

lives of animals in nature — not in unnatural captive
environments.

Endnotes

[1] People for the Ethical Treatment of Animals (PETA), "The Suffering Is Over at the Hawthorn Corporation!" https://www.peta.org/blog/hideous-hawthorn-corporation-history/ (Accessed January 1, 2022)

[2] Association of Zoos and Aquariums (AZA), "About AZA Accreditation." https://www.aza.org/what-is-accreditation (accessed January 1, 2022)

[3] Association of Zoos and Aquariums (AZA), "Species Survival Plan® Programs." https://www.aza.org/species-survival-plan-programs (accessed January 10, 2022)

[4] Smith, Roth. "Giraffe Killing at Copenhagen Zoo Sparks Global Outrage." National Geographic, February 11, 2014. Accessed January 10, 2022.

[5] Dell'Amore, Christine. "Copenhagen Zoo Kills 4 Lions After Controversial Giraffe Death." National Geographic, March 25, 2014. Accessed January 10, 2022.

[6] Horton, Helena. "Campaigners criticise European zoo proposals to cull adult male gorillas." The Guardian, November 26, 2021. Accessed January 10, 2022.

[7] Global Federation of Animal Sanctuaries, "Accreditation." https://www.sanctuaryfederation.org/accreditation/. Accessed January 10, 2022.